Peruvian Foreign Policy in the Modern Era

Ronald Bruce St John

ANTHEM PRESS

Anthem Press
An imprint of Wimbledon Publishing Company
www.anthempress.com

This edition first published in UK and USA 2023
by ANTHEM PRESS
75–76 Blackfriars Road, London SE1 8HA, UK
or PO Box 9779, London SW19 7ZG, UK
and
244 Madison Ave #116, New York, NY 10016, USA

British Library Cataloguing-in-Publication Data
A catalogue record for this book is available from the British Library.

Library of Congress Cataloging-in-Publication Data
A catalog record for this book has been requested.
2023931739

ISBN-13: 9781839982231 (Pbk)
ISBN-10: 1839982233 (Pbk)

Cover Credit: Photograph of Torre Tagle façade permission granted
by Ministry of Foreign Affairs of Peru.

This title is also available as an e-book.

To the Members of the Peruvian Diplomatic Service

CONTENTS

LIST OF FIGURES

ACKNOWLEDGMENTS

As Peru celebrates its bicentennial and I approach my 80th year, it seems the right time to conclude what has become a lifelong study of the foreign policy of Peru. Following the publication of several articles and reviews, I expanded my doctoral dissertation into a book on Peruvian foreign policy, *The Foreign Policy of Peru* (Lynne Rienner 1992). In 1999, the English language edition of the book was updated, translated into Spanish, and published as *La política exterior del Perú* by the Asociación de Funcionarios del Servicio Diplomático del Perú (AFSDP), an organization of active and retired Peruvian diplomats. Beginning with the Fujimori administration and concluding with the Boluarte government, *Peruvian Foreign Policy in the Modern Era* builds on the work contained in these earlier publications and will be my last book on the subject. I acknowledge that some of the information herein has appeared in one form or another in earlier publications; however, any material in the present work that I have published earlier has been revised, updated, expanded, or condensed as necessary to tell more fully the story of the foreign policy of Peru.

I first visited Peru in early 1968, the grateful recipient of a generous fellowship from the Shell Foundation for doctoral research in what was known at the time as a developing country. In the course of almost a full year of research and study in Peru, I lived through those tumultuous October days when a military junta headed by General Juan Velasco Alvarado (1968–75) overthrew the democratically-elected government of President Fernando Belaúnde Terry (1963–68). At the end of the year, I returned to the Graduate School of International Studies, now known as the Josef Korbel School of International Studies, at the University of Denver to complete my Ph.D. dissertation, entitled "Peruvian Foreign Policy, 1919–1939: The Delimitation of Frontiers." Shortly after my return, I had the opportunity in May 1969 to spend a day in the Denver area hosting *El Arquitecto* Belaúnde, as the university-trained architect and president-in-exile enjoyed being called, when he visited his son, a student at the Colorado School of Mines.

In the course of President Belaúnde's second term in office (1980–85), I enjoyed a long private interview with him in July 1983 in his offices in the Palacio de Gobierno. During a warm and animated conversation, he described his plans to build and develop his beloved Peru. As it turned out, our meeting took place on the same afternoon that the *Sendero Luminoso* guerrilla–terrorist movement blew up the Lima headquarters of Acción Popular, the political party founded and led by President Belaúnde. During our conversation, a presidential aide interrupted the meeting to whisper in the president's ear what had happened. President Belaúnde did not confide in me at the time what had transpired at party headquarters, where several people were killed or injured, nor did he interrupt the interview. Instead, he continued our discussion until he had finished outlining his plans for Peru, only then graciously albeit hurriedly excusing himself. I did not learn of the tragedy at Acción Popular headquarters until I returned to my apartment in Miraflores, a Lima suburb, later in the evening.

Like President Belaúnde, President Alejandro Celestino Toledo Manrique (2001–2006) was a visionary with ambitious long-term plans to develop Peru, gradually eliminating the world of poverty from which he originated. Both men recognized the need for roads, ports, and other infrastructure to be built to enable the Peruvian people to bring their goods to market and to participate more fully in the global economy. Over the years, President Toledo shared with me on multiple occasions his vision for Peru, material I later incorporated into a book on his administration entitled *Toledo's Peru: Vision and Reality* (University Press of Florida 2010). I count it a real tragedy that President Toledo, along with every Peruvian president between 1985 and 2023 save one, interim president Valentín Paniagua Corazao (2000–2001), has been impeached, imprisoned, or otherwise subjected to a criminal investigation.

Over more than five decades, I have incurred a countless number of debts, intellectual and otherwise, in Peru. For inspiration as well as practical assistance in those endeavors and this book, I would like to begin by thanking the late president Fernando Belaúnde Terry and former president Alejandro Celestino Toledo Manrique. Both men were very generous over the years with their time and the resources at their disposal.

I have also enjoyed the friendship, assistance, and support of a succession of Peruvian foreign ministers and deputy foreign ministers, including Eduardo Ferrero Costa, Arturo García García, Diego García-Sayán Larrabure, Efraín Goldenberg Schreiber, Luis Gonzales Posada, Víctor Ricardo Luna Mendoza, Oscar Maúrtua de Romaña, Luis Marchand Stens, Edgardo Mercado Jarrín, Augusto Morelli Pando, Hugo Ernesto Palma Valderrama, Javier Pérez de Cuéllar Guerra, José Eduardo Ponce Vivanco, Néstor Francisco Popolizio Bardales, José de la Puente Radbill, José Manuel Rodríguez Cuadros,

Alejandro San Martín Caro, Fernando Schwalb López-Aldaña, Fernando de Trazegnies Granda, Francisco Tudela van Breugel-Douglas, Jorge Valdez Carrillo, and Allan Wagner Tizón.

From the above group, I would like to acknowledge the support of Francisco Tudela van Breugel-Douglas, foreign minister and permanent representative of Peru to the United Nations in the 1990s as well as the first vice president of Peru for a brief period in the closing days of the Fujimori presidencies. Ambassador Tudela was a prime mover in the decision to translate *The Foreign Policy of Peru* into Spanish and its subsequent use in the curriculum of the Diplomatic Academy of Peru. I also want to offer a special thanks to Víctor Ricardo Luna Mendoza, the foreign minister of Peru (July 2016 – January 2018) during the Pedro-Pablo Kuczynski presidency. Ambassador Luna read and commented on Chapter 6, offering information and insight on the Kuczynski administration as well as on many other facets of contemporary Peruvian foreign policy.

Other Peruvian diplomats whose assistance has proved invaluable over the years include Juan Miguel Bákula Patiño, Augusto Bazán Jiménez, José Manuel Boza Orozco, Pedro Antonio Bravo Carranza, Oswaldo del Aguila Ramírez, Félix Calderón Urtecho, Rodolfo Enrique Coronado Molina, Manuel Augusto de Cossio Klüver, Gustavo Figueroa Navarro, Rosa Garibaldi de Mendoza, Ignacio Higueras Haro, Julio Estuardo Marrou Loayza, Gustavo Adolfo Meza-Cuadra Velázquez, María Cecilia Rozas Ponce de León, Augusto Ernesto Salamanca Castro, Ricardo Silva-Santisteban Benza, Olga Liliana Francisca de Olarte Paredes de Torres-Muga, and Juan Pablo Vegas Torres.

I would be remiss if I did not also thank the Ministry of Foreign Affairs of Peru for providing the photo of the Palacio de Torre Tagle, the Baroque palace built in the early 1700s which serves as its home and which provides a handsome cover for this book. Similarly, I want to acknowledge the International Boundaries Research Unit at the University of Durham for granting permission to reproduce two maps from my monograph, *The Ecuador-Peru Boundary Dispute: The Road to Settlement*, published in 1999. I also want to thank our son, Nathan Bailey St John, an architect and graphic artist working in Paris, for drawing the other five maps illustrating this book.

Peruvian academics, journalists and politicians whose warm friendship, as well as counsel and guidance, I have enjoyed and cherished over the years include Augusto Alvarez Rodrich, Manuel Burga Díaz, Percy Cayo Córdoba, Alejandro Deustua Caravedo, Lourdes Flores Nano, Claudia Izaguirre Godoy, Hélan Jaworski C., José Matos Mar, Sandra Namihas, Fabián Novak Talavera, Carlos Reyna Izaguirre, Oswaldo Sandoval Aguirre, Rosario

Santa Gadea Duarte, Pedro Ugarteche, Víctor Villanueva, and Ernesto Yepes del Castillo. Outside Peru, I would like to acknowledge Frank V. Ortiz, a former US ambassador to Peru, Stephen M. Gorman, David Scott Palmer, Howard Lawrence Karno, John Crabtree, Charles D. Kenney, Jennie K. Lincoln, Cynthia McClintock, and David Patrick Werlich for their influence on and support for my work over the many years.

A final note concerns the bibliography. In the course of a January 2014 lecture I gave at the Peruvian Diplomatic Academy in Lima, I was called out by a respected Peruvian scholar for not including several sources in the bibliography of *The Foreign Policy of Peru* that he felt were important to the study of Peruvian foreign policy. In response, I noted that the material available on the subject was so rich and varied that it was impossible to list in the bibliography more than the sources I had actually cited in the book. To avoid a repeat of this situation, I have entitled the bibliography "Works Cited."

On a personal level, I would like once again to acknowledge the encouragement and support of my wife, Carol, and our two sons, Alexander and Nathan. Much of the time I have devoted to academic endeavors over more than 50 years would otherwise have been theirs.

ABBREVIATIONS

ACE	Acuerdo de Complementación Económica (Complementary Economic Accord)
ALBA	Alternativa Bolivariana para las Américas, Alianza Bolivariana para los Pueblos de Nuestra América (Bolivarian Alternative for the Americas)
ALCA	Área de Libre Comercio de las Américas (Free Trade Area of the Americas)
AP	Acción Popular (Popular Action)
APEC	Asia-Pacific Economic Cooperation
APRA	Alianza Popular Revolucionaria Americana (American Popular Revolutionary Alliance)
ASPA	América del Sur–Países Árabes (South American–Arab Countries)
ATPA	Andean Trade Preferences Act
BRI	Belt and Road Initiative
CALC	Cumbre de América Latina y el Caribe (Latin American and Caribbean Summit)
CAN	Comunidad Andina de Naciones (Andean Community of Nations)
CDI	Carta Democrática Interamericana (Inter-American Democratic Charter)
CDS	Consejo de Defensa Sudamericana (South American Defense Council)
CELAC	Comunidad de Estados Latinoamericanos y Caribeños (Community of Latin American and Caribbean States)
CIDH	Corte Interamericana de Derechos Humanos (Inter-American Court of Human Rights)
CPTPP	Comprehensive and Progressive Agreement for Trans-Pacific Partnership
CSN	Comunidad Sudamericana de Naciones (South American Community of Nations)
EEU	Eurasian Economic Union
EFTA	European Free Trade Association
EU	European Union
EU-LAC	European Union, Latin America, and the Caribbean

FP	Fuerza Popular (Popular Force)
FTA	Free Trade Agreement
GDP	Gross Domestic Product
G-Rio	Grupo de Río (Rio Group)
ICJ	International Court of Justice
ICC	International Criminal Court
IDB	Inter-American Development Bank
IDC	Inter-American Democratic Charter
IIRSA	Iniciativa para la Integración de la Infraestructura Regional Suramericana (Initiative for Integration of Regional Infrastructure in South America)
IMF	International Monetary Fund
IU	Izquierda Unida (United Left)
JNE	Jurado Nacional de Elecciones (National Electoral Jury)
JP	Juntos por el Perú (Together for Peru)
LAFTA	Latin American Free Trade Association
MERCOSUR	Mercado Común del Sur (Southern Common Market)
MOU	Memorandum of Understanding
MRTA	Movimiento Revolucionario Túpac Amaru (Tupac Amaru Revolutionary Movement)
NAM	Non-Aligned Movement
OAS	Organization of American States
OECD	Organization for Economic Cooperation and Development
OEI	Organización de Estados Iberoamericanos (Organization of Ibero-American States)
PBEC	Pacific Basin Economic Council
PECC	Pacific Economic Cooperation Council
PL	Perú Libre (Free Peru)
PP	País Posible, Perú Posible (Possible Peru)
PPC	Partido Popular Cristiano (Popular Christian Party)
PPK	Peruanos Por el Kambio (Peruvians for Change)
PROSUR	Foro para el Progreso y Integración de América del Sur (Forum for the Progress and Integration of South America)
SADR	Sahrawi Arab Democratic Republic
SWAPO	South West Africa People's Organization
TPP	Trans-Pacific Partnership
UN	United Nations
UNASUR	Unión de Naciones Suramericanas (Union of South American Nations)
UNHRC	United Nations Human Rights Commission, United Nations Human Rights Council

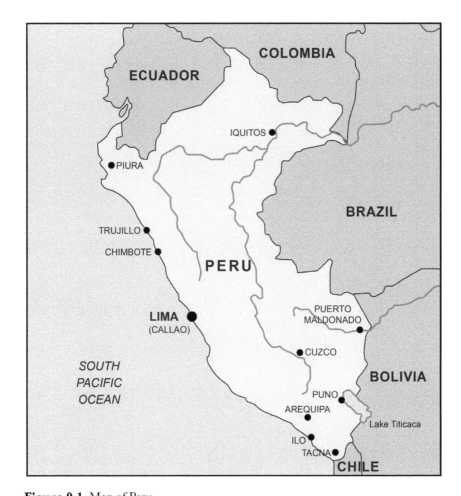

Figure 0.1 Map of Peru

Source: Nathan Bailey St John

Chapter 1

INTRODUCTION

The Republic of Peru enjoys a rich and storied history, and this is especially true when it comes to its external affairs. General José de San Martín in early August 1821, six days after he declared Peru independent, established the Ministry of State and Foreign Relations, appointing Juan García del Río as the first minister of foreign affairs of Peru. Following the decisive patriot victory at Ayacucho in 1824, Peruvian independence was finally secured, and the goals, capabilities, options, and constraints of Peruvian foreign policy began to clarify. In common with most of its neighbors, Peru from the outset focused on the accomplishment of a limited number of core objectives central to the well-being of any independent state, including political sovereignty, territorial integrity, continental solidarity, and economic independence.

With the exact location of its boundaries in dispute, Peru embraced the principle of *uti possidetis de jure de 1810* which generally stated that each new state was entitled to the territory formerly under the jurisdiction of the colonial administrative unit from which it was formed. Territorial issues were often complicated by the commercial advantages at stake as the coastal states of South America quarreled over trade routes and seaports. Ideological differences intensified all of these conflicts as did concerns for regional hegemony. Peru shared with neighboring states a profound awareness of interlocking interests, and bilateral disputes frequently assumed multilateral dimensions as states shifted alliances in search of relative advantage. The conflicting demands of independence and interdependence, as determined by this mix of domestic and international forces, strongly influenced the content and expression of Peruvian foreign policy over much of the next 200 years (Wagner de Reyna 1964, 1: 9–14).

End of the Beginning

Under President Ramón Castilla (1845–51, 1855–62), Peru first acquired the degree of internal peace, centralized and efficient state organization, adequate and reliable public funding, and an emerging sense of national unity necessary for the formation of a foreign policy. During his two terms in office, Peru experienced for the first time a government that outlined a foreign policy at the outset of its term and then worked to achieve its stated objectives. Articulating a coherent, comprehensive foreign policy founded on the principles of continental solidarity, nonintervention, and national integrity, Peru under Castilla assumed a leadership role in continental affairs. President Castilla was aptly supported in these endeavors by José Gregorio Paz Soldán, widely recognized as the most effective Peruvian foreign minister in the nineteenth century (Garibaldi de Mendoza 2003).

The 1860s was largely a decade lost in terms of advancing the central goals of Peruvian foreign policy; however, during the 1870s, Peru enjoyed a fresh opportunity to put its political and economic house in order and to regain the sense of direction and regional leadership achieved under Castilla. Unfortunately, the economic policies of the Manuel Pardo (1872–76) and Mariano Ignacio Prado (1876–79) administrations were not wholly successful and contributed to Peru's subsequent defeat in the War of the Pacific (1879–83) (Bonilla 1974, 127–90). After four long years of bloody fighting and protracted negotiations, the 1883 Treaty of Ancón reestablished peace between Peru and Chile. It was a punitive pact, with heavy indemnities, guaranteed to retard any improvement in regional relations. The provisions in the pact related to the final disposition of the Peruvian provinces of Tacna and Arica were particularly unfortunate because they constituted an open sore that poisoned hemispheric relations for decades to come (Palacios Rodríguez 1974). In the meantime, ongoing labor shortages led to new efforts at European immigration and ground breaking treaties with China and Japan. The 1873 treaty with Japan was Peru's first with an Asian state and Japan's first with a Latin American state (Morimoto 1999, 32–33). The 1874 agreements with China were noteworthy because they addressed the offensive coolie trade, a long-standing, and vexing problem for China and Peru (Stewart 1951, 175–76, 189–90).

Boundary Disputes, Development Capital, and Budding Nationalism

Chile remained the central issue on the foreign policy agenda of Peru in the postwar period. At the same time, Peru made progress in resolving complicated often interrelated boundary disputes with Bolivia, Brazil, Colombia, and Ecuador. Bilateral relations with the United States also improved. Given the economic and political ascendancy of the United States, Peru's ongoing need for development capital and diplomatic support clearly dictated better relations with Washington (Bonilla 1980, 71–105). The first administration of President Augusto B. Leguía (1908–12) accomplished several major achievements, including the resolution of the boundary disputes with Bolivia and Brazil, and during his second administration (1919–30), Leguía negotiated boundary settlements with Colombia and Chile. President Leguía emphasized the settlement of regional disputes in the belief that Peru's international credit, and his reputation as a statesman, would increase with their resolution (Ugarteche 1930, 69–93). Instead, his close association with North American interests, combined with his controversial territorial settlements, alienated influential segments of the population, nurturing the growth of a nascent Peruvian nationalism. The latent current of anti-United States feelings that had developed by the time Leguía was ousted in 1930 soon became a permanent part of the foreign policy environment of Peru (Clayton 1999, 104–41).

Over the next three decades, the challenges and opportunities of Peruvian foreign policy expanded in both scope and direction. Recognizing that modern diplomacy involved far more than the simple defense of the nation's frontiers, Peruvian diplomats expanded the breadth and depth of Peruvian foreign policy. With the apparent resolution in 1942 of the last remaining territorial issue, the boundary dispute with Ecuador, Peru resumed the leadership role in continental affairs that it had largely abandoned in the nineteenth century (Denegri Luna 1996, 251–89). The Peruvian government demonstrated a growing interest in Latin American economic cooperation and development and participated in multilateral conferences on maritime fishing and mineral resources. Peru was a founding member of the United Nations (UN) in 1945 and the Organization of American States (OAS) in 1948, and it joined the Latin American Free Trade Association (LAFTA) when it was created in 1960. Not satisfied with private sector investment as the principal means to generate economic development, Peru explored other sources for both financial and technical assistance, including the UN and the OAS. Tentative steps in the direction of an increasingly multilateral approach to foreign affairs paralleled a decline in the power and prestige of the United States in Peru (St John 1976, 325–44). After World War II, Peruvian foreign policy was characterized by a heightened sense of nationalism in which successive Peruvian governments displayed both the confidence and the capability to resolve international issues on their own terms (McClintock and Vallas 2003, 18–25).

New Directions

During the first term of President Fernando Belaúnde Terry (1963–68), Peruvian foreign policy began to move in new directions, addressing unfamiliar issues, adopting fresh approaches, and consummating new bilateral and multilateral relationships (Belaúnde Terry, interview with author, 16 May 1969). While Belaúnde appeared to match closely the specifications of the US government for democratic, socially progressive leaders able to carry the torch of the Alliance for Progress, a series of short and longer-term controversies with the United States came to a head during his first administration. Consequently, Peru faced a full or partial suspension of US economic aid during four of the five years Belaúnde was in office. At the same time, Belaúnde's efforts to implement reform programs often were undermined by mounting economic problems, many of which were created or accentuated by regime policies (Kuczynski 1977).

In October 1968, President Belaúnde was forced from office in a military coup d'état which led to 12 years of military rule, known as the *docenio*, under General Juan Velasco Alvarado (1968–75) and later General Francisco Morales Bermúdez (1975–80) (Aguirre and Drinot 2017). The foreign policy of the Velasco administration focused on two interrelated policies. It emphasized nationalism and anti-imperialism to generate domestic political support, and at the same time, it strived to reorder Peru's economic relationships with other states, especially the United States (Villanueva, interview with author, 14 July 1983; Jaworski 1984, 200–15). Inheriting severe economic problems, the Morales government in the second half of the decade reoriented Peruvian foreign policy, reemphasizing long-standing ties to neighboring states and rebuilding relations with the United States (St John 1992, 198–206).

In a time in which voters feared violence and had lost faith in the efficacy of revolution, Fernando Belaúnde Terry (1980–85) won reelection in 1980 on a platform of normalcy and gradual change. Therefore, it proved ironic that the Sendero Luminoso guerrilla–terrorist movement chose election day in 1980 to launch a people's war that would plague Peru for more than a decade (Roncagliolo 2018). The second Belaúnde administration also faced a number of geopolitical issues, including a reawaking of the border dispute with Ecuador, the UN Law of the Sea Convention (1982), the Malvinas (Falkland) Islands dispute between Argentina and Great Britain, and Bolivia's perennial search for a sovereign seaport on the Pacific. President Belaúnde hoped for a more positive relationship with the United States; however, the conflicting demands of Peruvian nationalism and the need for US cooperation to achieve core foreign policy goals made that impossible (Belaúnde Terry, interview with author, 11 July 1983). In the end, mounting economic concerns, including natural disasters, a growing insurgency, an expanding traffic in narcotics, and conflict within the ruling Acción Popular party proved more that President Belaúnde could manage. He left office with Peruvians facing the worst economic crisis of the century and quite possibly the worst in Peruvian history (St John 1992, 206–9).

In 1985, Alan García Pérez won a landslide victory on a promise to solve Peru's economic difficulties. Instead, he made matters worse. The García administration implemented a number of controversial economic policies, including a limit on interest payments on the external debt to 10 percent of export earnings, which collectively led both to record inflation levels and a deep recession. Over time, the foreign debt burden increased from US$14 billion in 1985 to more than US$23 billion in 1989, and Peru defaulted on some US$2 billion in International Monetary Fund (IMF) loans, making it one of the leading debtor nations in the world. By mid-1990, government expenditures were three times as large as government revenues, and the annual rate of inflation was in excess of 7,000 percent (Crabtree 1992, 25–68, 121–51). In the process, seemingly intractable economic problems repeatedly undermined key facets of Peruvian foreign policy.

In addition to advocating for greater arms control, pursuing better relations with Bolivia and Ecuador, and joining the Contadora Support Group, the García government took a more active role in the Non-Aligned Movement (NAM), established diplomatic relations with the South West Africa People's Organization (SWAPO) and supported efforts to end apartheid in South Africa (Ferrero Costa 1987, 55–78). At the same time, President García frequently employed strong language and a confrontational style with the US government, especially in the early years of his administration, over issues like the drug war, external debt, and Central America. In the end, the activist foreign policy of the García administration left little room for improvement in diplomatic relations with the United States (St John 1992, 209–13).

Concluding Observations

Beginning with the first Belaúnde administration, Peruvian foreign policy broadened in scope, interests, and relationships. Successive governments diversified arms transfers, expanded trade links, encouraged a radical reorientation of the inter-American system, and promoted enhanced regional and extra-regional cooperation. In a prolonged period of sustained innovation, each government naturally dealt with different challenges and opportunities; nevertheless, the general direction of Peruvian foreign policy reflected a continuity that transcended special interests or individual goals. In pursuit of heightened Peruvian sovereignty, every government from the first Belaúnde administration through the first García administration fought to reduce external pressures and imposed conditions, most notably from the US government. Concurrently, they promoted the territorial integrity of the state, working to resolve long-standing territorial issues with Bolivia, Chile, and

Ecuador. They also supported both regionalism and continental solidarity in part to achieve greater economic independence.

The following chapters pick up the story from here. Beginning with the election of Alberto Fujimori in 1990, the book examines the foreign policies of successive presidential administrations, concluding with that of Dina Boluarte. The focus of the analysis remains the permanent interests of Peru, political sovereignty, territorial integrity, continental solidarity, and economic independence, noting deviations from those permanent interests as they occurred. The theme of the book, as with my study of the earlier period, *The Foreign Policy of Peru* (1992), is the extent to which continuity and change have characterized Peruvian foreign policy since independence in 1824.

Chapter 2

ALBERTO KENYA FUJIMORI, 1990–2000 AND VALENTÍN PANIAGUA CORAZAO, 2000–2001

Alberto Fujimori, a little know university professor of Japanese descent, won the 1990 presidential election by a commanding majority. Following his election, Peruvian pundits referred to his campaign as a *tsunami*, a powerful metaphor highlighting the velocity and magnitude of his final electoral surge. With a straightforward campaign platform promising "Honesty, Technology and Work," Fujimori promised an era of socioeconomic and political reform. Instead, he presided over a decade of increasingly authoritarian rule, marked by a level of graft and corruption unknown in Peru.

Fujimori's election led to enormous change in countless areas of socioeconomic and political life, including the end of the traditional party system in Peru. In the 1980 presidential election, four political parties, Acción Popular (AP), Alianza Popular Revolucionaria Americana (APRA), Partido Popular Cristiano (PPC), and Izquierda Unida (IU), won 97 percent of the vote, and in the 1986 municipal elections, they took over 90 percent. The traditional parties appeared to be vibrant and robust; however, a weak electoral tradition, an inexperienced electorate, and the disappointing performance of traditional parties in office undermined their appeal. As the established parties were discredited, voters increasingly sought options outside the existing political system. Fujimori's victory in the June 1990 runoff sanctioned this decline. During the campaign, Fujimori created a new model of electoral organization known as the disposable party. Described by some observers as independent movements, disposable parties were seldom more than electoral labels or candidate-centered vehicles. Over the next three decades, the decline in traditional political parties, combined with the rise of disposable parties, had a significant influence on both the domestic and the foreign policies of Peru (Tanaka 1998, 59–235).

The Five D's

Given the deplorable state of the Peruvian economy, the first priority of the Fujimori government was to improve relations with the international financial community. Before his inauguration, President-elect Fujimori traveled to Japan and the United States, promising to implement an austerity program and resume service on the external debt. In response, an international consortium, including Japan, Spain, and the United States, made a preliminary commitment for bridge loans to cover the defaulted debt to the IMF and other multilateral lending agencies. Less than two weeks after his inauguration, President Fujimori announced the initial phase of a stern economic stabilization program. Dubbed *Fujishock*, it was based largely on the orthodox economic policies he had denounced during the campaign. Central elements of the program included a liberalization of foreign trade policies, deep cuts in tariff rates, and the lifting of import restrictions. Overnight, the government ended price controls and subsidies in place for decades. Thereafter, the Fujimori administration mostly followed orthodox economic policies in a largely successful effort to restore the international standing of Peru (Iguíñez 1998, 24–40).

President Fujimori viewed US government support as essential to any attempt to restore the international standing of Peru. Consequently, he focused initially on the issues of drug production and trafficking, the policy areas of most interest to Washington. With Peruvians more concerned with combating guerrilla–terrorist movements than they were with the drug war, President Fujimori's approach highlighted the early pragmatism of his government (Luna Mendoza, interview with author, 1 September 1999). The US government expected Peru to agree quickly to a substantial infusion of US military assistance to combat the drug problem; however, the Fujimori administration rejected a July 1990 proposal to that effect, arguing the drug problem could not be solved by military means alone. Instead, the Fujimori government proposed an alternative approach that addressed the drug issue but stressed economic as opposed to military solutions. The Peruvian proposal, which was the basis for a 1991 agreement between Peru and the United States, responded more fully to economic, political, and social issues in Peru than the US approach and represented an early diplomatic victory for the Fujimori government. In May 1995, Peru and the United States concluded a new five-year agreement to promote alternative development and economic growth in coca-growing zones, and in 1996, they replaced the 1991 pact with a new joint commitment to fight drug trafficking (St John 1999b, 213; McClintock and Vallas 2003, 117–18, 122–24, 128–29).

The issues of drug production and drug trafficking were the touchstones of bilateral relations between Peru and the United States throughout the

Fujimori era; however, US foreign policy toward Peru had a broader focus. In common with US policy throughout much of Latin America, US policy toward Peru in the 1990s focused on the so-called five d's: *las drogas, la democracía y derechos humanos, el desarrollo económico, la deuda*, and *la defensa* (drugs, democracy and human rights, economic development, debt, and defense). Washington's agenda in Peru was similar to that throughout the region with the emphasis varying from country to country depending on the challenges and opportunities faced by the United States (Palmer 1998, 25–30).

Democracy and human rights in Peru, a concern in Washington throughout the 1980s, increased in scope and intensity in the 1990s (Youngers 2006). Enjoying consistently high approval ratings, President Fujimori in April 1992 executed an *autogolpe* (self-coup), suspended the 1979 constitution, padlocked the congress, and dismantled the judiciary. He then announced that democracy would be suspended temporarily in order to build new institutions. His approach to restructuring the political regime further undermined institutional checks and balances already inadequate for the protection of human rights (Kenney 2004, 171–260). In October 1992, Fujimori dismissed 117 Peruvian diplomats, challenging the traditional professionalism of the Ministry of Foreign Affairs, increasing his interference in Peruvian diplomacy and subordinating the institution to his vision of the world. In the interim, security forces captured the founder of Sendero Luminoso, Abimael Guzmán, crippling a guerrilla–terrorist movement that disputed the very existence of the state for more than a decade (Roncagliolo 2018, 117–31).

While a growing number of Peruvians approved of Fujimori's policies, especially his stabilization of the economy and success against guerrilla–terrorists, his popularity did not silence criticism of alleged human rights abuses. Official statements critical of the state of human rights in Peru, like the State Department's annual report on human rights, were augmented by reports from NGOs, like Amnesty International and Human Rights Watch, detailing specific cases (McClintock and Vallas 2003, 142–47; Ramacciotti and Méndez 2012, 105–6, 108–10). In Washington, the George H. W. Bush administration (1989–93) condemned the autogolpe but refused to implement broad economic sanctions on Peru for fear that they would jeopardize the war against terrorism. In a cable to the State Department just three months after the autogolpe, the US Ambassador to Peru, Anthony C. E. Quainton, concluded that "Peru is heading in a direction which is consistent with our long-term interests" (Quiroz 2008, quoted on 372).

President Fujimori appeared to win 64.42 percent of the vote in the 1995 presidential elections and a majority in the newly created unicameral legislature. His closest competitor, Javier Pérez de Cuéllar, a widely respected, two-term UN Secretary-General, received 21.81 percent of the vote.

Pérez de Cuéllar was supported by PPC and a fraction of the left. The remaining three traditional political parties, AP, APRA, and IU, collectively polled a paltry 6.32 percent of the vote. The party system in Peru collapsed between 1989 and 1992, and the 1995 election ratified its demise (Tanaka 2001, 65–76). While Fujimori won big in 1995, it was not the overwhelming victory he proclaimed. The 1993 constitution changed the basis upon which election percentages were calculated from total votes cast, including blank and spoiled votes, to valid votes only. When abstentions as well as blank and spoiled votes were taken into account, Fujimori's 64 percent of total votes was reduced to only 39 percent of valid votes. Similarly, his party's 52 percent majority in Congress was reduced to only 18.5 percent of the total electorate, hardly a mandate for the controversial legislation that followed the 1995 election (Palmer 1995, 17–20).

With the increase in economic and political stability, the Fujimori government was able to gradually reinsert Peru into the international financial community and begin to address issues of debt and development. Stabilization policies ended a prolonged period of hyperinflation, economic growth increased, privatization advanced, exports grew, and foreign investment responded positively to new investment laws. Efforts toward economic normalization culminated in a Paris Club agreement in July 1996 in which Peru restructured most of the US\$9.25 billion owed to official creditors. Economic growth slumped later in the decade, first due to the *El Niño* weather pattern and Asian financial crisis and later because of the resulting global financial turmoil (Iguíñez 1998, 24–40).

Defense was the fifth and final element of US policy toward Peru in the 1990s. As with many aspects of that policy, implementation of the defense component proved paradoxical. After Fujimori rejected the initial US aid package in late 1990, the Bush administration responded to the autogolpe by suspending all military aid and most economic assistance. For the remainder of the decade, the limited security cooperation that did occur was tainted by graft and corruption, blocking any prospect for sustained security cooperation (Stone 2002, 45–49).

Subregional, Regional, and International Cooperation

In South America, the formal movement toward greater subregional and regional cooperation began during the first Belaúnde administration when Chile, Colombia, Ecuador, Peru, and Venezuela in the 1966 Declaration of Bogotá committed themselves to the negotiation of an economic integration agreement. Three years later, Bolivia, Chile, Colombia, Ecuador, Peru, and later Venezuela concluded the 1969 Cartagena Agreement, establishing the Andean Group. The Velasco administration enthusiastically supported the Cartagena Agreement; however, the support of subsequent Peruvian governments wavered. The second Belaúnde administration (1980–85) reaffirmed Peru's commitment to subregional cooperation, but its approach to national development goals slowed progress toward Andean integration (Avery 1983, 156–65). Similarly, the first García administration (1985–90) was committed to the ideal of Latin American unity, but it was unable or unwilling to pursue the bold initiatives required to resolve the mounting crises faced by the Andean Group (St John 1999b, 201, 204; Prado 2015, 159, 164–65).

In the beginning, the Fujimori government was an enthusiastic supporter of expanded subregional cooperation and development. President Fujimori presided over the opening meeting of the Andean Parliament when it convened its eighth ordinary session in Lima in February 1991, and in May, he joined other Andean leaders in calling for talks with the US government to discuss trade, investment, environmental, and drug trafficking issues. Andean leaders also urged the US Congress to pass a bill under discussion which encouraged Andean agricultural workers to replace coca production with farm products exportable to the United States under preferential terms. In so doing, the Fujimori government highlighted the importance it assigned to a broad approach to the drug war that addressed both issues of drug production and trafficking and the economic development needs of the rural areas in which coca was grown. Under pressure from Peru to move forward with Andean integration, the Andean presidents in late 1991 concluded the Acta de Barahona (Barahona Act), establishing a free trade zone in 1992 and implementing a common external tariff in 1992–94 (St John 1996, 131–32; Seoane Flores 2000, 295–96).

The fallout from the 1992 autogolpe dealt a severe blow to Andean Group efforts at subregional cooperation just when the movement seemed to be gaining momentum. In August 1992, Peru announced its withdrawal for two years from active participation in the Andean Group, and a few weeks later, Peru opposed a common external tariff. By early 1994, the Fujimori administration was planning for full reintegration into the Andean Group by June 1995; however, an armed clash with Ecuador in January 1995 later delayed plans for tariff reductions and thus full-scale reentry into the Group (St John 1999b, 218–20). Overall, the period 1992–97 was one of some tension between Peru and the Andean Group, renamed the Comunidad Andina de Naciones (CAN) in 1997, in which Peru struggled to reconcile domestic and CAN economic policies. After announcing in 1997 that it was separating from CAN, Peru later resumed talks with its Andean neighbors and its participation in CAN affairs (Prado 2015, 162–63, 165–67).

As the decade progressed, the Fujimori administration was increasingly active in the Asia-Pacific region. President Fujimori capitalized on his Japanese heritage to promote trade and investment, especially with China, Japan, and South Korea (Morimoto 1999, 213–25). In the case of China, the US dollar value of Peruvian exports to China increased almost fivefold in the decade after 1993 and imports from China increased more than sevenfold. Fujimori eventually visited China four times in the course of his decade in power (Zanabria 2015, 90). Peru joined the Pacific Basin Economic Council (PBEC) in 1990, the Pacific Economic Cooperation Council (PECC) in 1991, and the Asia-Pacific Economic Cooperation (APEC) forum in 1998 (Hooker 2015, 193–94). When the Movimiento Revolucionario Túpac Amaru (MRTA) guerrilla–terrorist movement attacked the Japanese ambassador's residence in mid-December 1996, seizing 72 hostages, Fujimori authorized a commando raid in which all the guerrillas were killed (González Vigil 2012, 225–27). Widely popular in Japan, President Fujimori made his tenth visit to Japan in 1999, marking the 100th anniversary of the first wave of Japanese emigration to Peru (McClintock and Vallas 2003, 38, 74–75).

Elsewhere, the Fujimori administration also pushed for stronger international ties, especially with the European Union (EU). Throughout the decade, Peru moved to increase financial and technical cooperation with the EU in a variety of areas, including health care, investment, judicial reform, and trade. At the same time, the Fujimori government continued to cultivate bilateral investment and trade ties with important European states, notably France, Germany, and Spain (Novak 2012, 175–82, 187–92, 195–98; Novak and Namihas 2016, 37–59). In June 1999, Peru also participated in the first summit of heads of state and government of the European Union–Latin America and the Caribbean (EU-LAC), a new strategic partnership aimed at improving understanding in the political, economic, and cultural spheres (Valdez Carrillo 2012, 166–67).

Territorial Issues

Following its temporary withdrawal from the Andean Group, Peru negotiated bilateral trade agreements with neighboring states, including Colombia, Ecuador, and Venezuela. In addition, the Fujimori administration in January 1992 concluded a 50-year renewable agreement with Bolivia in which Peru agreed to provide Bolivia with a duty-free port and an industrial park at the Peruvian port of Ilo, 1,260 kilometers south of Lima and 460 kilometers west of La Paz. In return, Peru received similar facilities at Puerto Suárez on the Paraguay River where Peru hoped to increase trade with Argentina, Brazil, and Paraguay. Peru also ceded to Bolivia a tourist zone for 99 years, together with five kilometers of Ilo coastline. In addition, the bilateral agreement provided an Inter-American Development Bank (IDB) loan for infrastructure development in and around the port of Ilo (Novak and Namihas 2020, 176–79; St John 2020, 150).

Bolivians had aspired to a sovereign port on the Pacific Ocean since independence in 1825, and they immediately baptized the coastal strip Boliviamar while in Peru it was generally referred to as Bolivia Mar (Figure 2.1). At the same time, Bolivia was quick to emphasize that it viewed the event as simply another step in Bolivia's intent to recover its full rights to the sea (Araníbar Quiroga, interview with author, 13 March 2001). In turn, Peru stressed the need, while respecting existing international agreements, to pursue creative, pragmatic solutions to difficult regional problems. Over the next decade, Bolivia and Peru expanded the original Ilo agreements in a series of pacts intended to promote the duty-free Bolivian facility at Ilo. Other arrangements created the Lake Titicaca Binational Agency to promote the joint development of the Lake Titicaca Basin, including the Desaguadero River, Lake Popoó, and the Salar de Coipasa. In 1998, Bolivia and Peru also concluded an MOU that provided for private entities to construct a gas pipeline from La Paz to Ilo (Novak and Namihas 2013, 169–73; St John 2020, 150–51). As for the original Ilo agreement, early Bolivian enthusiasm for Bolivia Mar soon subsided and the tourist zone was never developed.

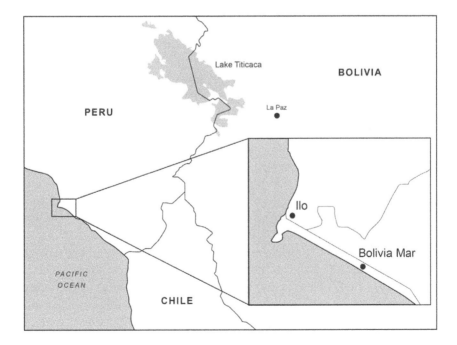

Figure 2.1 Bolivia Mar

Source: Nathan Bailey St John

Thirty years later, the five-kilometer strip of land that Peru ceded to Bolivia for 99 years remained a deserted beach (*La República*, 20 January 2022).

In 1992, the Fujimori government initiated a new round of negotiations with Chile aimed at the full implementation of the 1929 Tacna and Arica Treaty and Additional Protocol. In May 1993, Chile and Peru concluded the Convenciones de Lima (Lima Conventions) which were thought to have resolved this long-standing dispute (St John 1994, 24–25). Less than two years later, the foreign ministers of Chile and Peru agreed to set aside the 1993 agreements and seek "a practical and concrete formula" related to the facilities and freedom of transit the 1929 agreements provided for Peru at the Chilean port of Arica (Tudela van Breugel-Douglas, interview with author, 31 August 1999). Over the next four years, Peru was preoccupied with the Ecuadorian border dispute, and little progress was made on the issue. In the interim, Chile and Peru signed a free trade agreement in mid-1998 that removed tariffs on some 2,500 products with duties on others to be phased out over a 3- to 18-year period (St John 1999b, 221; Novak 2000, 42–53).

After almost a year of often tough negotiations, the foreign ministers of Chile and Peru in November 1999 signed a package of documents that executed the 1929 agreements, ending 70 years of controversy. Central elements of the Acta de Ejecución (Act of Execution) addressed a requirement in Article 5 of the 1929 treaty that called for Chile to construct for Peru a wharf, customs office, and railway terminal at Arica and a requirement in Article 2 of the additional protocol that called for Peru to enjoy absolute freedom of transit of persons, merchandise, and armaments to and from Peruvian territory. In addition, the agreements recognized the right of servitude, as detailed in Article 5 of the 1929 treaty, including its application to the Arica and Tacna Railway Company where it crossed Chilean territory (Novak 2000, 57–178; St John 2000, 97–98). At the same time, Chile agreed to return to Peru some 200 books and documents, mostly pertaining to the city of Tacna, that Chilean forces had looted during the War of the Pacific. Foreign Minister Fernando de Trazegnies Granda, an author and dedicated bibliophile, drew enormous personal satisfaction from this relatively minor provision in the 1999 settlements (De Trazegnies Granda, interview with author, 2 September 1999).

After more than a decade of relative quiet on the border, the armed forces of Ecuador and Peru in January 1995 again clashed in the most serious round of fighting since 1941. With neither side able to achieve a decisive military solution, the Fujimori administration in mid-February 1995 initiated a diplomatic offensive that led to a ceasefire (Palma Valderrama 2022). At that point, Ecuador recognized the 1942 Rio Protocol was still in effect, reversing the nullity thesis it had articulated since 1960. In turn, Peru showed flexibility

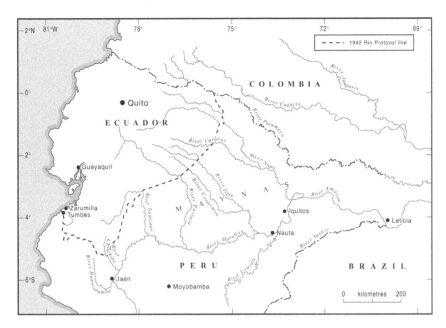

Figure 2.2 Rio Protocol line

Source: IBRU, Durham University, UK

in its long-held position that the Rio Protocol was a final solution to the dispute, acknowledging that a disagreement still existed that impeded demarcation of the border. In February 1995, Ecuador and Peru, together with the four guarantors of the 1942 Rio Protocol (Argentina, Brazil, Chile, and the United States), signed the Declaración de Paz de Itamaraty, accords that focused on ending the fighting, stabilizing the frontier and initiating the process of demarcating the border (Tudela van Breugel-Douglas 2019, 95–113) (Figure 2.2).

After a sustained diplomatic effort lasting over three years, the guarantors of the 1942 Rio Protocol in October 1998 announced a Global and Definitive Peace Agreement known as the Brasilia Accords (Ferrero Costa 2018). The agreement delimited the boundary line on the summit of the Cordillera del Cóndor and created two national parks in the frontier zone under the sovereignty and jurisdiction of the respective states (Figure 2.3). Ecuador also received one square kilometer of ground in Peru on the point designated as Tiwinza, the site of heavy fighting in 1995; however, this transfer of land did not entail any "consequences as to sovereignty" with Ecuador enjoying real title except the right to transfer the property. Finally, the agreement called on Ecuador and Peru to formalize treaties on trade and navigation, border integration, and free trade as well as to exchange diplomatic notes on the Napo River, Zarumilla Canal, and a binational commission on mutual

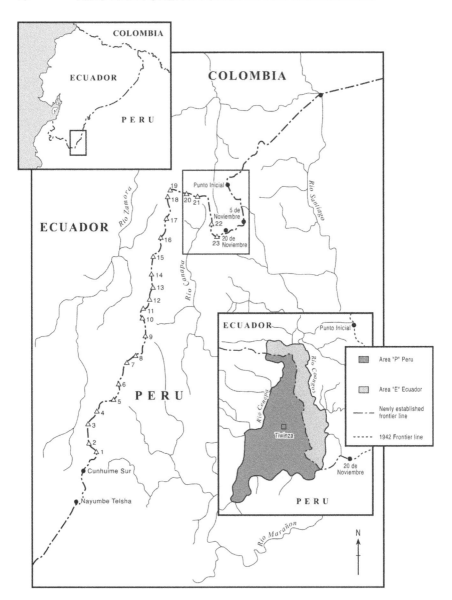

Figure 2.3 Boundary markers in the Cordillera del Cóndor

Source: IBRU, Durham University, UK

confidence and security. In October 1998, the IDB announced a US$500 million loan for the economic and social development of the frontier zone, the first installment in a US$3 billion international commitment to develop the Ecuador–Peru borderland. Demarcation of the Ecuador–Peru border was completed in May 1999 (St John 1999a, 30–49; Bákula 2002, II: 1344–67).

End of the Road

Despite widespread improbity and venality that trampled on human rights, compromised domestic policies, and eviscerated state institutions, the Fujimori government enjoyed more success in advancing core objectives of Peruvian foreign policy than any other government in the second half of the twentieth century. President Fujimori restructured the foreign debt on terms highly favorable to Peru, restoring the nation's standing in the international financial community and setting the stage for the pursuit of a more autonomous national development policy. Regional and extra-regional cooperation increased, relations with important Asia-Pacific states expanded, and by the end of the decade, bilateral relations with the United States were the most positive in recent memory. Finally, the full implementation of the Tacna and Arica Treaty and Additional Protocol completed a process begun in 1929, and the final resolution of the Ecuador–Peru border dispute on terms highly favorable to Peru achieved a goal of successive Peruvian governments since independence.

Interim Paniagua Administration, 2000–2001

Once the graph and corruption of the Fujimori administration became public knowledge, pro-Fujimori politicians lost control of the congress, and President Fujimori fled to Japan, faxing a letter of resignation on 20 November 2000. Following the resignation of both the first and the second vice presidents, constitutional succession passed to Valentín Paniagua Corazao, president of the congress. On 22 November 2000, he was sworn in as the president of Peru for an interim, transitional period until a new president could be elected (Paniagua Corazao, interview with author, 16 March 2001). President Paniagua immediately turned to Javier Pérez de Cuéllar, an esteemed diplomat, to form an interim cabinet. In addition to serving as prime minister, Pérez de Cuéllar also assumed the portfolio of foreign minister (Pérez de Cuéllar 2012, 145–47).

Prime Minister Pérez de Cuéllar considered the reinsertion of Peru into the international community as the interim government's most important foreign policy objective. Consistent with this goal, the Peruvian delegation to the Third Summit of the Americas in Quebec in April 2001 proposed the Carta Democrática Interamericana (Inter-American Democratic Charter, CDI), a document grounded in the OAS Charter. Ambassador Manuel Rodríguez Cuadros, Peruvian ambassador to the OAS at the time and a future foreign minister of Peru, was the architect of the CDI which was later adopted by the OAS General Assembly (Rodríguez Cuadros, interview with author, 14 March 2008; Negro 2012, 282–83). The interim government also moved to normalize relations with international bodies, like the International Criminal Court (ICC) and the Corte Interamericana de Derechos Humanos (Inter-American Court of Human Rights, CIDH), which were anathema to the Fujimori administration. It also worked closely with the Andean Community. In addition, Prime Minister Pérez de Cuéllar visited neighboring states, including Argentina, Chile, Colombia, and Ecuador, and he moved to reform personnel practices within the Ministry of Foreign Affairs related to the mistreatment of professional diplomats in the Fujimori era (Pérez de Cuéllar 2012, 148–49; St John 2022, 202–3, 206).

Chapter 3

ALEJANDRO CELESTINO TOLEDO MANRIQUE, 2001–2006

Alejandro Toledo rose from humble beginnings in the north of Peru to earn an undergraduate degree at the University of San Francisco and graduate degrees at Stanford University. In the 2001 presidential race, most of the candidates, including Toledo, were centrist, pro-market, and emphatic about their democratic credentials. Stressing his indigenous roots and rise from poverty, Toledo occupied the center ground between former president Alan García Pérez, a center-left populist, and Lourdes Flores Nano, a center-right conservative. Toledo defeated García in the second round with 53.08 percent of the vote (St John 2010, 27–31, 37–38).

Unlike its predecessors, the Toledo administration articulated an interrelated set of foreign policy goals at the beginning of its term in office and then pursued them over the next five years. First, it continued the long-time Peruvian emphasis on expanded integration with subregional, regional, and international organizations. Second, it emphasized better relations with the industrialized states of the world as well as the major powers in the Asia–Pacific region. Third, it promoted democracy and human rights, often tying improvement in these areas to a fourth policy goal, the struggle against poverty. Fifth, it advocated reduced arms spending throughout the region, arguing the money would be better spent on education, health care, and poverty reduction. Sixth, it worked to improve diplomatic and commercial relations with neighboring states, encouraging economic development in the borderlands. Seventh and eighth, it called for the Ministry of Foreign Affairs to promote the domestic economy abroad and to improve services to the more than two million Peruvians living overseas. Finally, the Toledo administration encouraged ongoing reforms at the Ministry of Foreign Affairs (García-Sayán Larrabure 2002, 18–27; Toledo Manrique, interview with author, 12 September 2008).

Subregional and Regional Integration

In his 2001 inaugural address, President Toledo promised a foreign policy that would connect Peru with the outside world, emphasizing the need to expand relations with subregional, regional, and international organizations. He called for CAN to be relaunched to accelerate regional integration, and he urged member states to adopt a multilateral approach to arms control, using the savings achieved to expand social welfare programs (Toledo Manrique 2001). In late 2002, CAN concluded a free trade agreement with the Mercado Común del Sur (Common Market of the South, MERCOSUR), and in March 2003, it agreed to work with the Área de Libre Comercio de las Américas (Free Trade Area of the Americas, ALCA) and the EU to pursue a joint strategy against poverty, drugs, and terrorism (MREP 2006a, 42).

In November 2003, Ambassador Allan Wagner, a long-time proponent of regional integration, was elected secretary-general of CAN. Thereafter, the Toledo administration assumed a leadership role in the organization with Wagner arguing that a higher level of integration would encourage solutions to regional issues like the Chile-Peru maritime dispute (*Expreso*, 1 July 2004). During Peru's tenure as president pro tempore of CAN (2004–2005), the UN General Assembly's decision in September 2004 to create an Andean Peace Zone free of biological, chemical, and nuclear weapons was a noteworthy achievement (St John 2010, 165–66).

In April 2006, Venezuelan President Hugo Chávez, a vocal critic of the market reform and free trade policies advocated in the so-called Miami Consensus, withdrew from CAN after Colombia and Peru concluded free trade agreements with the United States. Chávez then joined Fidel Castro and Bolivian President Evo Morales in forming what became the Alternativa Bolivariana para las Américas (Bolivarian Alternative for the Americas, ALBA), a socialist alternative to ALCA (Philip and Panizza 2011, 1–12, 149–73). ALBA's activities were heavily dependent on Venezuelan oil rents, and Chávez's death in March 2013, followed by severe economic problems under President Nicolás Maduro, exposed its core fragility. Well over a decade after its creation, ALBA remained more a concept that a concrete integration effort (Bilotta 2018, 7–10).

The Comunidad Sudamericana de Naciones (South American Community of Nations, CSN), created in December 2004 and renamed the Unión de Naciones Suramericanas (Union of South American Nations, UNASUR) in April 2007, initially targeted a gradual convergence of CAN and MERCOSUR (MREP 2006c, 235–40). While ALBA and UNASUR reflected divergent domestic and geopolitical aspirations, both sought an alternative to the neoliberal paradigm expressed in the Washington Consensus

(Bilotta 2018, 1, 10–13). CSN appeared to offer a path to reconciling any conflict between Peruvian membership in CAN and its associate membership in MERCOSUR; consequently, Peru at the outset was an enthusiastic supporter of CSN. Moreover, the emphasis CSN placed on physical integration through the Iniciativa para la Integración de la Infraestructura Regional Suramericana (Initiative for Integration of Regional Infrastructure in South America, IIRSA), a multinational initiative comprising 10 axes or hubs of economic integration crisscrossing the South American continent, dovetailed with Peruvian aspirations to become a regional hub for Pacific South America (Adins 2015, 249–50).

Global Initiatives

In a policy distinct from its predecessors, the Toledo administration encouraged major reforms to important international institutions. In the spring of 2003, Ambassador Wagner, foreign minister for a second time in 2002–2003, expressed concern about what he termed a "fractured" international system. In response, he spearheaded a Grupo de Río (Rio Group, G-Río) initiative to reform the UN collective security system. The proposed reforms included an increase in the number of Security Council members, elimination of the veto power of the five permanent members, and revisions to the collective security system to better manage threats to international peace (Wagner Tizón, interview with author, 9 May 2003). The Cusco Consensus, a joint statement issued at the end of the May 2003 G-Río summit, identified the strengthening of democratic governance as the primary G-Río mission and called for UN reforms similar to those identified earlier by Foreign Minister Wagner (St John 2003).

At the same time, the Toledo administration championed familiar issues like democracy, human rights, and reduced arms spending in international forums. In mid-September 2001, only two months after Toledo's inauguration, the OAS General Assembly adopted the CDI. Core elements of the CDI later found their way into the 2003 Cusco Consensus. In April 2002, the UN Human Rights Commission (UNHRC) adopted a Peruvian resolution that defined the central elements of democracy as respect for human rights, freedom of association, and free elections based on universal suffrage. In October 2005, Peru was elected a nonpermanent member of the UN Security Council for 2006–2007, a position it last held in 1984–85. Around the same time, the Toledo administration initiated a campaign to ratify the Convención de las Naciones Unidas sobre el Derecho del Mar (United Nations Convention on the Law of the Sea, CONVEMAR). In January 2006, Peru assumed the presidency of the UNHRC, and in May, it was elected to the newly-created UN Human Rights Council (UNHRC) (St John 2010, 173).

Elsewhere, the Organización de Estados Iberoamericanos (Organization of Ibero–American States, OEI), an organization comprised of the heads of state of Latin America, Portugal, and Spain, met in Lima in November 2001. At the meeting's end, the participants issued the Declaración de Lima (Lima Declaration), a statement in support of democracy, human rights, and reduced arms spending that largely mirrored the domestic and foreign policy agenda of the Toledo administration. At the third OEI summit in November 2003, Peru won support for a Toledo administration proposal to allow debtor nations to reduce debt payments, investing instead in infrastructure projects (Rodríguez Cuadros, interview with author, 14 March 2008). At the Extraordinary Summit of the Americas in January 2004, one of the few noteworthy proposals adopted was a Peruvian initiative, the Declaración de Nuevo León (Nuevo León Declaration). It affirmed that the well-being of the peoples of the Americas required social development, equitable economic growth, and democratic government. Peru also attended the first summit of América del Sur-Países Árabes (South American–Arab Countries, ASPA) which met in mid-2005 (Ayuso et al. 2018, 62). The organizers of the summit considered it a historical gathering, but former foreign minister Rodríguez Cuadros offered a more sober assessment. He noted the idea behind the meeting was positive but little noteworthy was accomplished (Rodríguez Cuadros, interview with author, 14 March 2008).

Strengthening Ties with the United States

The return of democracy to Peru opened both challenges and opportunities in its conflicted relationship with the United States. Having spent years studying and working in the United States, President Toledo knew the country well and appreciated its power. In turn, the US government viewed the election of Toledo as an opportunity to build on the relationship it had developed with the Fujimori administration. In March 2002, President George W. Bush became the first sitting US president to make an official visit to Peru (McClintock and Vallas 2003, 161). During his stay, Bush reiterated an earlier US pledge to triple aid to combat drug trafficking, announced the Peace Corps would return to Peru after almost three decades and reaffirmed his commitment to renew the Andean Trade Preferences Act (ATPA). He also expressed the hope that the case of Lori Berenson, a New York woman retried and convicted in June 2001 of collaborating with the MRTA guerrilla–terrorist movement, could be referred to the CIDH. Outside Peru, human rights groups and others protested her confinement, but inside Peru, a large swath of the population had little sympathy for her (Ramacciotti and Méndez 2012, 120–21).

Even as bilateral relations strengthened, the Toledo administration took foreign policy decisions that were unpopular in Washington (Maúrtua de Romaña, interview with author, 18 April 2006). With public opinion in Peru overwhelmingly opposed to the March 2003 US-led invasion of Iraq, President Toledo refused to support it on the grounds it had not been approved by the UN Security Council. The war on drugs was another source of discord with the US government rejecting Peru's argument that narco-trafficking was a regional issue necessitating a regional solution. Over time, trade tensions also increased with Peru arguing the Bush administration was holding progress in bilateral negotiations hostage to the resolution of outstanding disputes with US companies (Toledo Manrique, interview with author, 19 April 2006). Another source of tension was the Peruvian refusal to accede to US demands that US citizens be shielded from ICC prosecution in a so-called bilateral immunity agreement (St John 2010, 177–78). Finally, President Toledo in November 2004 publicly endorsed a CIDH decision that Lori Berenson must serve out her prison term (Berenson 2005; Ramacciotti and Méndez 2012, 121–27).

Despite these policy differences, the Toledo government was able to maintain a strong working relationship with the Bush administration. Mid-way through his presidency, President Toledo described the chemistry of his personal relationship with President Bush as a level of closeness to skin itself (Toledo Manrique, interview with author, 9 May 2003). At a time when populist, socialist regimes in Bolivia, Ecuador, and Venezuela increasingly offered alternatives unwelcome in Washington, the Bush administration embraced the Peruvian approach to the promotion of democracy, human rights, and free trade (McClintock and Vallas 2010, 197, 199). Presidents Bush and Toledo clearly developed a strong personal relationship, albeit not one without its critics. "Some say Peru is the unconditional ally of the United States," José Carlos de la Puente Radbill, a former foreign minister, wryly observed in the course of a conversation; however, "it might be better to be an ally with conditions" (De la Puente Radbill, interview with author, 9 May 2003).

Stronger Relations with Europe and Asia

Recognizing the importance of maintaining strong relations with the industrialized world, President-elect Toledo completed a three-week tour of Europe, including stops in France, Germany, Spain, and Strasbourg, seat of the European Parliament, before his inauguration (St John 2010, 175). In December 2002, the EU agreed to provide Peru with €86 million in financial aid to support improved governance, stronger institutions, socioeconomic development, and integration, and in June 2005, Lima was chosen as the site for EU-LAC 2008. In addition to developmental assistance, the EU supported the Toledo administration in other areas, including drug control and judicial reform (Novak and Namihas 2016, 59–77). The Toledo government also expanded relations with individual European states, including Belgium, France, Germany, Great Britain, Italy, Russia, and Spain. Germany was especially generous, designating Peru as a country for so-called concentrated cooperation and extending €89 million in bilateral aid in 2002–2006 (MREP 2006b, 30–31; Novak 2012, 183–85, 192–93, 198–203).

The Fujimori administration had expanded ties in the Asia-Pacific region, and the Toledo administration continued this shift in Peruvian foreign policy. In 2004, Peru granted China market economy status, and later in the same year, China reciprocated, granting Peru approved destination status. In January 2005, China and Peru concluded agreements related to agriculture, tourism, and energy exploitation. Six months later, President Toledo traveled to China, met with President Hu Jintao, and signed agreements on education, health, tourism, and transportation (Fuentes Cervantes 2018, 43). Peru opened a consulate in Guangzhou in September 2005, and in October, China and Peru signed an MOU which covered cooperation in technological information and communications (MREP 2006b, 32, 50). Stressing the importance of China to Peru, President Toledo once commented in a jocular manner that he was not overly ambitious in regards to China and would be satisfied with 5 percent of the China market (Toledo Manrique, interview with author, 19 April 2006).

President Toledo hoped to build on the strong relationship with Japan developed by his predecessor; however, the Japanese government's reluctance to extradite former president Fujimori proved a difficult hurdle to overcome. When Fujimori in November 2005 flew from Japan to Chile and announced plans to return to Peru to run in the 2006 presidential elections, Chilean authorities arrested him (Maúrtua de Romaña, interview with author, 18 April 2006). Two months after President Toledo left office, Fujimori was finally extradited from Chile to Peru to face multiple charges. Elsewhere in the region, the Toledo administration concluded a free trade agreement with Thailand in November 2005, and in February 2006, the two states signed an air transport agreement. In November 2005, South Korea and Peru exchanged ratifications for an extradition treaty, and in February 2006, Peru opened a resident embassy in Vietnam (MREP 2006a, 85–86; MREP 2006b, 32, 50).

Neighboring States

During the Toledo administration, bilateral relations with Ecuador focused on mutual efforts to fulfill the terms of the Brasilia Accords. Unfortunately, international aid commitments never reached the target of US$3 billion over 10 years nor did aid disbursements match aid commitments. In turn, the growth in bilateral trade was steady albeit slower than anticipated (García-Sayán Larrabure, interview with author, 11 March 2008). Over time, agreements on a variety of issues, from conservation to sanitation to drugs, were concluded or implemented as bridges, roads, electrical networks, and other facilities were upgraded or constructed. Bilateral and multilateral investment in the borderlands also continued with Peru performing significantly better than Ecuador in this regard (Arróspide del Busto, interview with author, 13 March 2008; Novak and Namihas 2010, 35–62).

During Toledo's five years in office, Bolivia had six presidents, and their political philosophies ranged from the far right to the far left. In this volatile milieu, most of the issues addressed by the Toledo administration, namely economic integration, labor migration, tourism, and trade, carried over from the Fujimori government. A number of pacts were signed in 2001–2006, but the dominant issue remained the Peruvian port of Ilo as an exit for Bolivian natural gas (Novak and Namihas 2013, 196–217). In January 2002, Presidents Toledo and Jorge Quiroga Ramírez inaugurated a new international bridge at Desaguadero and floodgates to regulate the waters of Lake Titicaca. During their meeting, Toledo reiterated Peruvian interest in being the exit port for Bolivian gas. The Toledo administration again raised the issue in August 2002 following the inauguration of President Gonzalo Sánchez de Lozada, proposing to route the gas through a pipeline parallel to the La Paz-Desaguadero-Ilo road (Wagner Tizón, interview with author, 9 May 2003). Bolivia eventually rejected the Peruvian proposal on the grounds it did not include a sovereign outlet to the Pacific (Sánchez de Lozada, interview with author, 9 September 2003). In August 2004, Presidents Toledo and Carlos Diego Mesa Gisbert, who replaced Sánchez de Lozada in October 2003, signed a letter of intent for Bolivian natural gas to be exported to Mexico and the United States through an unspecified Peruvian port. The terms of the pact led to widespread protests in Bolivia, resulting in President Mesa's resignation in early June 2005 (García-Corrochano 2012, 82–83; St John 2020, 151–52, 157).

The December 2005 election of Juan Evo Morales Ayma strained Peru–Bolivia relations, putting them on hold for the remainder of the Toledo administration (St John 2006a). Morales was the first democratically elected Bolivian president of indigenous heritage, and while his patrimony might suggest an affinity with Toledo, deep philosophical differences separated the two men. Where Toledo encouraged orthodox economic policies and free market reforms, Morales questioned the benefits of globalization, advocating nationalization and socialism. Where Toledo negotiated a free trade agreement with the United States, Morales concluded people's trade agreements with Cuba and Venezuela. Where Toledo expanded ties with regional and international trade and finance organizations, Morales looked to the alternative trade and finance structures promoted by Venezuelan President Chávez. Where Toledo cultivated bilateral ties with industrialized states, notably the United States, Morales allied with a smaller number of mostly left-leaning states, like Cuba, Nicaragua, and Venezuela (St John 2020, 171–84, 193–96). Finally, President Toledo rejected the populist appeal of Morales, denouncing populism "as a one-night party that inevitably will end up in a funeral" (Toledo Manrique, interview with author, 19 April 2006).

In August 2003, President Toledo and Brazilian President Luiz Inácio Lula da Silva concluded a wide-ranging strategic alliance. First, they agreed to promote increased cooperation and development within the framework of IIRSA. Second, they agreed to promote bilateral trade and investment within the context of the Acuerdo de Complementación Económica (Complementary Economic Accord, ACE) between Peru and MERCOSUR. Third, Brazil agreed to negotiate Peruvian access to two surveillance systems it was developing in the Amazon Basin to provide both meteorological data and real-time information on illegal activities. Other goals of the strategic alliance included support for democracy and the rule of law, the promotion of human rights as a central element of socioeconomic development, and the creation of improved conditions for friendship, understanding, commerce, and transit (Novak and Namihas 2012, 123–55; St John 2016, 147–49). Foreign Minister Wagner, an experienced and highly professional diplomat not given to hyperbole, described the strategic alliance with Brazil as the most important event in Peruvian foreign policy in the last 30 years (*Gestión*, 26 August 2003).

Bilateral relations with Colombia centered on national security issues with the two states concluding several agreements aimed at combating terrorism, drug trafficking, and arms smuggling. To reduce military spending and better prioritize social spending, they also worked to improve economic opportunities in the borderland (Maúrtua de Romaña, interview with author, 18 April 2006). As investment and trade increased, they concluded an innovative agreement that called for both states to treat air travel in the borderland as domestic travel, simplifying customs and tariff procedures (MREP 2006a, 77; Namihas 2012, 60, 63).

President Toledo was a strong advocate of reduced military spending; consequently, Chilean arms purchases were a persistent issue after 2001 (Maúrtua de Romaña, interview with author, 18 April 2006). An increasingly acrimonious dispute over the Chile-Peru maritime boundary further complicated relations. In addition to national pride, the dispute involved thousands of square kilometers of the Pacific Ocean, rich fishing grounds, and other potentially important undersea resources (Rodríguez Cuadros 2007). With Chile and Peru adopting fundamentally different positions on the issue,

President Toledo eventually decided to take it to the International Court of Justice (ICJ) at The Hague (St John 2010, 153–55). Before the Court, Peru argued that no agreed upon maritime boundary existed between Chile and Peru and asked "the Court to plot a boundary line using the equidistance method in order to achieve an equitable result." In addition, Peru contended that "beyond the point where the common maritime boundary" ended, it was "entitled to exercise exclusive sovereign rights over a maritime area lying out to a distance of 200 nautical miles from its baselines." (This area is hash marked on Figure 3.1). Chile argued that the "Declaration on the Maritime Zone" signed by Chile, Ecuador, and Peru in Santiago on 18 August 1952 "established an international maritime boundary along the parallel of latitude passing through the starting-point of the Peru-Chile land boundary and extending to a minimum of 200 nautical miles" (ICJ 2014, 15).

On a more positive note, the Toledo administration succeeded in negotiating a so-called social agenda with Chile, addressing social security, health care, and other concerns of Peruvians living in Chile and Chileans working in Peru (García-Corrochano 2012, 80–81).

At the end of the interim Paniagua government, diplomatic relations with Venezuela reached a low point over Peruvian charges that Venezuelan

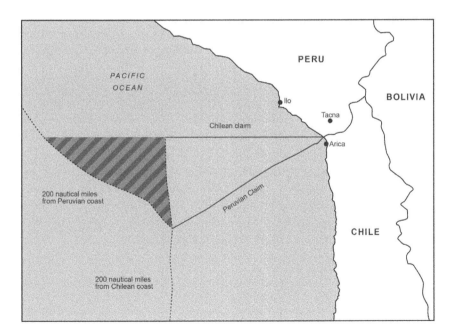

Figure 3.1 Maritime Claims of Chile and Peru

Source: Nathan Bailey St John

officials were shielding Vladimiro Montesinos, a central figure in the vast web of illegal activities under former president Fujimori. After Montesinos was detained in June 2001, President Chávez accused Peru of violating Venezuelan sovereignty, suggesting it was seeking to discredit his self-styled revolution (*El Comercio*, 18 July 2001). Conflict more than cooperation remained the hallmark of bilateral relations between Peru and Venezuela during the Toledo years; nevertheless, bilateral trade continued to grow with the balance in Venezuela's favor (St John 2010, 158–59).

Social Diplomacy and Institutional Reform

Under Toledo, social diplomacy for the first time became a stated goal of Peruvian foreign policy even though core elements of the concept were not new (Maúrtua de Romaña, interview with author, 18 April 2006). States like Peru have long recognized that governments must focus resources on helping citizens to combat poverty through increased participation in multilateral bodies concerned with socioeconomic development. Ambassador Manuel Rodríguez Cuadros, either vice minister or minister of foreign affairs for 50 of the 60 months Toledo was in office, was an especially strong proponent of social democracy, arguing diplomacy must serve the Peruvian people (Rodríguez Cuadros, interview with author, 14 March 2008). With some 10 percent of the population living outside Peru, the Toledo government also worked to improve services for this substantial expatriate population (Tapia Samaniego 2011, 22–25, 43–49, 71–77).

During the Toledo administration, the Ministry of Foreign Affairs continued many of the personnel reforms initiated by the interim Paniagua government (Novak and Namihas 2020, 184–86). After congress set new standards for the diplomatic corps, including a diplomatic clause that stated that in the future no one in the Ministry should be expected to obey an authoritarian government, 51 of the 117 diplomats arbitrarily and unconstitutionally dismissed by the Fujimori administration in 1992 were reinstated. Of the remaining 66 diplomats, a few had been reinstated earlier and others had passed the mandatory retirement age or died (García-Sayán Larrabure 2002, 220–34, 241–45; St John 2022, 202–3, 206).

Conclusions

President Toledo brought enthusiasm, energy, and boldness to the foreign policy of Peru. The strategic alliance with Brazil and the bilateral relationship with the United States would not likely have progressed to the extent they did without his vision and leadership. At the same time, very few countries in or out of Latin America were as successful as Peru in saying "no" to the Bush administration. The Toledo government also pursued more traditional, less glamorous, policy initiatives, like borderland development with Ecuador, subregional integration with Bolivia, and a solution to the maritime dispute with Chile. In pursuit of its goal to better connect with the outside world, the Toledo administration was a highly visible, often effective player in regional and international organizations, and relations with China and other Asian states reached new heights. Not always successful, the diplomacy of the Toledo administration most often showed dexterity, persistence, and professionalism in dealing with involved, interrelated, and often long-standing issues. In so doing, the foreign policy of the Toledo administration connected Peruvians to the outside world to a far greater extent than any previous government, strengthening the credibility and global reputation of the state.

Chapter 4

ALAN GARCÍA PÉREZ, 2006–2011

Having left office in 1990 with the lowest approval rating in Peruvian history, former President Alan García Pérez, a brilliant orator and protégé of the legendary APRA leader, Victor Raúl Haya de la Torre, reinvented himself in the course of the 2006 presidential campaign. Billing himself as an elder statesman who had learned from past mistakes, he targeted his message at younger Peruvians with no memory of his disastrous first administration. During the campaign, García promised "responsible change," embraced the neoliberal model and positioned himself as a defender of the status quo (St John 2006b; Crabtree and Durand 2017, 1, 125–26). In the first round of the 2006 election, García came in second behind Ollanta Humala Tasso, a populist retired army officer, but in the second round, García overtook Humala, winning the presidency with 52.8 percent of the vote (St John 2006c).

Peru experienced strong economic growth during the second García administration; nevertheless, government policies were slow to reduce poverty levels, leaving the majority of Peruvians increasingly unhappy (*Economist*, 12 May 2008). President García also failed to address pressing social issues, like indigenous rights, corruption, drug trafficking, and human rights, and his attempts to open the Amazon rainforest to exploitation and development led to spirited indigenous protests. In the highlands, indigenous elements protested living and working conditions at multiple large mining sites, including La Oroya, considered one of the 10 most polluted places in the world. Additional sources of discontent included coca farmers opposed to coca eradication efforts, informal miners rejecting efforts to integrate them into the formal economy, and splinter groups of the Sendero Luminoso guerrilla–terrorist movement active in remote regions of the country (*La República*, 4 June 2011). Constrained by limited popularity and the absence of a legislative majority, the García administration appeared largely content with strong macroeconomic figures, ignoring the paradox between economic growth rates among the highest in the region and dysfunctional governance. President García focused on his coastal base mostly ignoring the interior and failing to bridge deep socioeconomic divides in a country marked by severe inequality and widespread social discontent (St John 2006d).

Blending Old and New

In his 28 July 2006 inaugural address, President García stressed domestic issues. When it came to foreign policy, he pledged to maintain economic development and economic growth at rates equal to or greater than that of his neighbors. Promising his government would maintain a global focus, he pledged to reduce presidential travel abroad, reflecting criticism that President Toledo had spent too much time outside Peru (St John 2006d). Consistent with García's emphasis on government thrift, the Ministry of Foreign Affairs announced plans to close six embassies, a symbolic rejection of Toledo's promotion of a more visible international role for Peru. Ironically, President García later was criticized for not traveling abroad enough (Álvarez Rodrich, interview with author, 12 March 2008).

Prior to his inauguration, President-elect García told Andrés Oppenheimer, a syndicated columnist in Miami, Florida, that "Peru's foreign policy has not been the most misguided part of Toledo's government. So, we must continue with [current policies] in issues such as opening up to the world market and drawing investments in a framework of democracy" (*Miami Herald*, 11 June 2006). In office, the foreign policy of the second García administration blended the old and new, often mirroring the policies of President Toledo. For example, both Toledo and García viewed counter narcotics policy as largely synonymous with counter insurgency policy, a change in part due to an evolution in guerrilla–terrorist strategy. With the capture of Abimael Guzmán in 1992, Sendero Luminoso gradually lost its ideological bearings and became more of a narco-terrorist organization (McClintock and Vallas 2010, 207). In an August 2006 media interview, Foreign Minister José Antonio García Belaúnde was mildly critical of Toledo's foreign policy but then outlined a set of goals little changed from it (*La República*, 3 August 2006).

During the second García administration, support for market-friendly policies replaced the emphasis on socialism in the first García government, and after questioning the free trade agreement with the United States during the 2006 election campaign, President García embraced it once in office (St John 2006d). In addition, the two governments shared similar views on economic development, drug trafficking, democracy, and security (McClintock and Vallas 2010, 201–10). President García never developed the close personal relationship with Presidents George W. Bush and Barack Obama that Toledo enjoyed with Bush; nevertheless, his multiple visits to the White House were an achievement for someone who was in effect persona non grata in Washington by the end of his first term (MREP 2011, 74–75, 116, 219–20; Ramacciotti and Méndez 2012, 127–36). In 2010, Peru welcomed the return of pre-Columbian artifacts taken from Machu Picchu in 1912 by the US archeologist and historian Hiram Bingham and held by Yale University's Peabody Museum for almost 100 years (*El Comercio*, 20 November 2010).

Subregional, Regional, and International Cooperation

In a June 2006 interview, President-elect García emphasized that his government would focus on a wider South American union, emphasizing that Brazil was central to a broader relationship with the region (*Perú21*, 9 June 2006). In November 2006, President García completed a two-day official visit to Brazil to consolidate the strategic alliance negotiated by his predecessor, and in February 2008, he was the first head of state to visit Brazil following President Luiz Inácio Lula da Silva's election to a second term, signing 12 new accords on technical cooperation, health, education, biotechnology, energy, and Amazon security. In May 2008, President Lula made an official visit to Peru, concluding 10 pacts, and in June 2010, Presidents García and Lula met in Manaus where they signed 12 agreements, including accords on education, energy, finance, and health. Bilateral meetings at all levels of government also occurred throughout the García presidency with the emphasis always on the full implementation of the strategic alliance concluded by the Toledo government (MREP 2011, 46–47, 68–69, 108–9, 156–59, 211–12). By the end of the second García administration, Peru had exceeded the number of presidential visits and agreements with Brazil completed by the Toledo government, suggesting the strategic alliance with Brazil would continue to develop independent of changes of government in either country (De Zela 2012, 31–41; Novak and Namihas 2012, 155–87).

The second García administration supported regionalism in general and UNASUR in particular; however, its enthusiasm for the latter was noticeably less than that of the Toledo government. Of the nine presidential summits organized by CSN and UNASUR in 2006–11, for example, President García attended only three. Moreover, Peru was often in the minority on policy issues addressed by UNASUR, including the 2009 elections in Honduras and the candidacy of Néstor Kirchner, former president of Argentina, as secretary general of UNASUR. Peru remained outside the Banco del Sur, constituted in 2007, and expressed reservations over the original Brazilian proposal to create the Consejo de Defensa Suramericano (South American Defense Council, CDS). On the positive side, the second García administration formulated a proposal in 2009 calling for a Protocolo de Paz, Seguridad y Cooperación (Protocol of Peace, Security, and Cooperation) with objectives that included the reduction of armament expenditures in the subregion, confidence building, demining, and the creation of a peace force capable of intervening in subregional conflicts. The proposal reflected long-held Peruvian interests but failed to generate the necessary consensus among UNASUR member states (MREP 2011, 58, 89, 136, 188, 239–41, 284; Adins 2015, 150–52).

Although the García administration continued the policies of Presidents Fujimori and Toledo in a variety of regional and international bodies, it did not pursue certain initiatives in areas like the promotion of democracy and the reduction of regional arms expenditures as aggressively as the Toledo government (MREP 2011, 183–87, 233–35). On the other hand, President García embraced many of the policies of the Toledo government in areas like social diplomacy and improved services to Peruvians abroad. Foreign Minister García Belaúnde later noted with some pride that Peru in 2011 had 108 consuls or consular sections abroad plus 136 honorary consuls (García Belaúnde, interview with author, 14 January 2014; Tapia Samaniego 2012, 25–32).

Throughout the second García administration, Peru continued to build on its asymmetric relationship with the European Union. By any measure, including area, population, GDP per capita, or balance of trade, the partnership was unequal with the EU the dominant player. The most significant development in this relationship was the conclusion in October 2009 of an MOU establishing a bilateral consultative mechanism between the EU and Peru with the objective of increasing cooperation and understanding between the two bodies. The agreement provided for an annual meeting at the vice minister of foreign relations level at which topics, as varied as strengthening the state and justice system, human rights, sustainable development, and tourism, were discussed. Peru also concluded a number of bilateral agreements with the EU on a variety of subjects, including cooperation in science and technology, migration, narco-trafficking, and strengthening democracy. Finally, the EU member states remained the single largest investors in Peru contributing approximately 50 percent of total investments with the United States in second place (Novak and Namihas 2016, 77–109).

In the Middle East, the García administration maintained good relations with Israel but also pursued wider relations with the Arab World. Peru sent its first ambassador to Qatar, recognized the Palestinian State as sovereign and independent, and opened trade talks with the six Arab Gulf states (García 2012, 243–69). In April 2010, Foreign Minister García Belaúnde completed a swing through the Middle East, visiting Bahrain, Kuwait, Qatar, Saudi Arabia, and the United Arab Emirates, and a second trip in October 2010 included stops in Egypt, Jordan, Lebanon, Libya and Syria (Novak and Namihas 2020, 213–14). In addition, Peru participated in the first and second summits of South American–Arab Countries and hosted the third one which was delayed until October 2012 because of the Arab Spring and the resultant instability in the Arab World (MREP 2011, 176–78, 228–29, 278–79; Ayuso et al. 2018, 62–64).

Asian Initiatives

With China, the second García administration augmented the initiatives put in place by the Toledo government, building on existing agreements in areas like education, health, trade, and transportation (Marczak 2010). Peruvian exports to China continued to grow, and visits between Chinese and Peruvian leaders were a frequent occurrence, including official visits by President García to China in 2008 and 2010. During his 2008 visit to Beijing, García expressed Peruvian support for two issues of great importance to China: nonrecognition of Taiwan and Chinese control over Tibet (*El Comercio*, 28 March 2008). In 2007, Peru and China began negotiating a free trade agreement, and in 2008, they elevated their relationship to a strategic partnership (MREP 2011, 78–79, 123–24, 173, 224–25, 277).

Ongoing participation in APEC forums helped Peru to conclude free trade agreements with Canada and Singapore in 2008 and China in 2009. To build on its relationship with China, Peru linked the free trade agreement to their strategic partnership which in 2013 was elevated to a comprehensive strategic partnership (Alden and Méndez 2019, 286; Novak and Namihas 2020, 209–10 221–24). At the same time, Peru took advantage of its geographical location to promote itself as a regional hub for South America (Fuentes Cervantes 2018, 43–45). In 2010, the García government concluded a free trade agreement with the European Free Trade Association. In 2011, it signed a free trade agreement with South Korea and a commercial agreement with Japan (MREP 2011, 78–80, 124–25, 174–75, 225–27, 278; González Vigil 2012, 236–40).

Finally, President García promoted the creation of what was initially branded as an *Arco del Pacífico* (Pacific Arch) but later became the *Alianza del Pacífico* (Pacific Alliance) (Novak and Namihas 2018a, 23–27). At the very end of the second García government, Chile, Colombia, Mexico, and Peru in April 2011 formally agreed to launch the Pacific Alliance, a regional trade agreement formally established in June 2012 (*La República*, 10 February 2012). Subsequently, the presidents of the Pacific Alliance in a joint declaration on 8 October 2013 announced the conclusion of negotiations removing all trade barriers between the four member states, creating the eighth largest economy in the world (Nolte and Wehner 2013, 1–2).

Borderland Developments

Diplomatic and commercial relations with Ecuador continued to focus on the full implementation of the 1998 Brasilia Accords with an emphasis on their borderlands. After the first Ecuador-Peru binational cabinet meeting in 2007, a mechanism Peru would quickly adopt with other neighbors, binational committees and commissions met on a regular basis, and several conventions addressing details of the 1998 agreement were signed (León Collazos 2018, 2). The November 2006 election of Ecuadorian president Rafael Correa provided the García government with a willing partner to advance their common agenda (Novak and Namihas 2010, 22–74). In May 2011, Peru and Ecuador clarified their common maritime space, establishing the geographical parallel passing through the Boca de Capones as the maritime boundary and recognizing the Gulf of Guayaquil as a historic bay. At the same time, Ecuador and Peru agreed that agreements signed by Chile, Ecuador, and Peru in 1952 and 1954 which regulated the continental shelf and insular seas were fishery agreements and not boundary settlements (*Caretas*, 5 May 2011; Novak and Namihas 2020, 190–91). In the dispute with Chile, Peru had long argued that the 1952 and 1954 treaties were fishing agreements; consequently, the 2011 agreement with Ecuador strengthened Peru's position in its maritime dispute with Chile. (MREP 2011, 48–49, 70–72, 111–13, 161–62, 180–81, 214–16, 270, 281; De Trazegnies Granda 2012). Foreign Minister García Belaúnde later stated that the maritime agreement with Ecuador was one of the most important achievements of his time in office (*Caretas*, 3 June 2011).

Early on in President García's second term, Peru finalized a free commerce agreement with Chile largely negotiated by the Toledo administration. It also concluded a bilateral agreement covering domestic employees working in the country of the other. Nevertheless, the disposition of former president Fujimori remained a contentious issue well into the coming year, and in the end, the Chilean Supreme Court did not authorize Fujimori's extradition to Peru until September 2007 (Burt 2008). Concerning the maritime issue with Chile, President García supported the Toledo administration's decision to take the question to the ICJ, appointing two-time foreign minister Allan Wagner as the agent for Peru (MREP 2009; García Belaúnde 2014). In an interview after he left office, Foreign Minister García Belaúnde noted that Chile seemed amenable to compromise on minor issues early in President García's second term in the apparent hope it would forestall a Peruvian decision to take the maritime issue to the ICJ. Once Peru took that decision, Chile was noticeably more intransigent on core issues like regional arms control (García Belaúnde, interview with author, 14 January 2014).

Like Ecuador, Peruvian foreign policy with Colombia focused largely on borderland issues, including economic development, increased commercial exchange, and improved collaboration against narco-trafficking. Most of these issues involved questions of national security; consequently, the ministers of foreign affairs and defense of Colombia and Peru met on a regular basis in so-called 2+2 meetings. In July 2008, Presidents García, Lula of Brazil, and Álvaro Uribe Vélez of Colombia signed a tripartite MOU intended to combat narco-trafficking in the Amazon region, and in March 2011, President García completed a state visit to Colombia (MREP 2011, 69–70, 110–11, 160–61, 179–80, 213–24, 269–70; Namihas 2012, 55–73).

Foreign Minister García Belaúnde also made some progress in improving bilateral relations with Bolivia. Early on, Bolivia's reluctance to accept the modifications to the CAN agreement required to implement Peru's free trade agreement with the USA and its refusal to negotiate a common CAN trade agreement with the EU frustrated Peruvian officials (Valdez Carrillo 2012, 170–74). As late as June 2009, Bolivian president Morales, in a critique of the capitalist system, described Presidents Bush and García as the "peores presidentes del mundo" (world's worst presidents) (*La República*, 23 June 2009), and in August 2009, Foreign Minister García Belaúnde described President Morales as "un enemigo declarado del Perú" (a declared enemy of Peru) (*La República*, 30 August 2009). In an effort to improve relations, García Belaúnde in late 2009 appointed former foreign minister Rodríguez Cuadros to serve as the Peruvian ambassador to Bolivia. As soon as he arrived in his new post, Ambassador Rodríguez Cuadros endorsed Bolivia's demand for an exit to the sea (*El Comercio*, 19 February 2010). In mid-October 2010, the first 2+2 meeting of the foreign and defense ministers of Peru and Bolivia took place, and one day later, Presidents García and Morales signed a complementary protocol to the 1992 Bolivia Mar agreement, providing Bolivia with a duty free zone and access to Peruvian port facilities at Ilo. Over the coming months, additional meetings on borderland development, the common management of Lake Titicaca, and related issues took place as the García government strived to improve bilateral relations with Bolivia (MREP 2011, 45–46, 68, 107, 155, 210–11, 230–31; García-Corrochano 2012, 81–94; Novak and Namihas 2013, 217–33).

In a time of mounting international concern for the world's freshwater resources, the Mauri (Maure) River dispute with Bolivia resurfaced during the García administration. For more than a century, Peru had been diverting water from the Mauri River and its tributaries to the Pacific coast for irrigation, water supply, and more recently, mining projects. After 1970, Peru initiated or expanded several projects that increased the transfer of water from the upper basin of the Mauri River to the coast. By 2002, the current rate of extraction had led to a significant loss of wetlands and a deterioration in water quality in Bolivia, including elevated levels of arsenic and boron (*El Diario*, 9 November 2002). At that point, Bolivia took the position that any Peruvian attempt to divert additional water from the Mauri River must take into account both the rights of downstream users and the evolving law on transboundary water resources (*El Diario*, 30 May 2009). In 2003, Bolivia and Peru formed a joint commission to determine the maximum amount of water that could be diverted without affecting Bolivia (Alurralde Tejada et al. 2011, 5–6, 14). Over the years, the commission was unable to reach a consensus decision, and in 2010, the two parties implemented binational hydrometric stations to monitor water sharing of the Mauri River (Autoridad Nacional del Agua 2015, 16–28, 122–59; St John 2020, 192–93).

Venezuelan Meddling

During the 2006 presidential campaign, President García traded barbs with President Hugo Chávez after the latter termed García "a swine, a gambler, and a thief" and characterized President García and former president Toledo as "two alligators from the same swamp" (McClintock 2006, quote 104). Critical of Presidents Chávez and Morales during the presidential campaign, García tried to reach out to them after his election in an effort to calm the rhetoric. At the same time, he cast his government as the antithesis of Chávez and Morales, arguing in the course of a Washington, DC visit that a bilateral free trade pact was necessary to thwart the threat of Andean Fundamentalism in South America (*Washington Post*, 10 October 2006). During Ecuadorian president Correa's January 2007 inauguration, Presidents García and Chávez met and agreed to renew diplomatic ties, temporarily ending the rift that had begun during the 2006 presidential campaign (*La República*, 15 January 2007). In March 2008, Peruvian police arrested nine people alleged to be militants bankrolled by Venezuela, and the García administration again accused Chávez of meddling in the domestic affairs of Peru (*Miami Herald*, 22 March 2008). In the end, recurrent tensions with Venezuela proved a difficult balancing act for President García, hampering any diplomatic reconciliation (MREP 2011, 49, 73, 85–86, 272).

Conclusions

A seasoned diplomat, Ambassador José Antonio García Belaúnde was the foreign minister of Peru during the entire second presidency of Alan García Pérez, the first person in Peruvian history to serve in that capacity throughout a full five-year presidential administration. To add perspective to García Belaúnde's tenure and contribution to Peruvian diplomacy, it is instructive to recall that the Toledo administration had five foreign ministers in five years, and in the July 2020 to July 2021 period, Peru had five foreign ministers in 365 days. When asked if the foreign policy of the García administration mirrored that of the Toledo government, Ambassador García Belaúnde took a moment to reflect before giving a thoughtful response. "So, I would say that we had more clear ideas [than the Toledo administration] but not necessarily different," adding "we were less ideological, less biased, than Toledo" (García Belaúnde, interview with author, 14 January 2014). When asked about former president Fujimori and his delayed extradition from Chile to Peru, García Belaúnde argued that the Toledo administration's forceful approach to the issue had unduly soured relations with Chile and Japan. Consequently, the primary goals of the García administration included the normalization of relations with both Chile and Japan as well as with Bolivia and Venezuela, and in the end, it made considerable progress toward those goals. Ambassador García Belaúnde also noted what he characterized as the tendency of the Toledo administration to promise more than Peruvian diplomacy could deliver. In turn, he suggested Brazil, China, and Japan were three countries in which the second García administration succeeded in advancing diplomatic relationships.

Chapter 5

OLLANTA HUMALA TASSO, 2011–2016

Taking a page from his predecessor, retired army officer Ollanta Humala Tasso reinvented himself during the 2011 presidential campaign. In 2006, he was a fiery populist, donning red shirts, boasting plans to establish state control over natural resources, criticizing US policies, and touting support from Hugo Chávez and Evo Morales. Five years later, Humala had become a moderate, pro-business social democrat who often wore a business suit. Moreover, Nadine Heredia Alarcón de Humala, the candidate's charming and photogenic wife, was never far from his side—or from the cameras. Brazilian political consultants were central to Humala's transformation from a radical politician into a socially moderate one, attractive to a broader political base and international markets (Aramayo and Pereira 2011; St John 2016, 153). Humala won the first round with 31.7 percent of the vote followed by Keiko Fujimori, daughter of former president Alberto Fujimori, who polled 23.6 percent. In the second round, Humala was elected with 51.54 percent of the vote (Lupu 2012).

Three factors helped to explain Humala's surprising victory. First, the collapse of political parties in Peru led to a fragmented political environment. Ten candidates ran for president in 2011 but only five were truly competitive. Three establishment candidates together won 44 percent of the vote, but none of them won enough votes to move to the second round, opening the door to anti-establishment candidates to advance. Second, despite the economic boom under García, public discontent and distrust of the political system was high due to a weak state and weak democratic institutions. Concerned about crime and corruption, the electorate voted for change. Third, Humala's moderate turn during the campaign, masterminded by Brazilian advisers, helped him win over middle class voters. Fujimori, on the other hand, was unable to distance herself from the authoritarian government of her imprisoned father (McClintock and Vallas 2011).

In most important areas, the foreign policy of the Humala administration closely resembled the foreign policies of the Toledo and García governments. In an interview, Foreign Minister Rafael Roncagliolo Orbegoso rightly emphasized that "the foreign policy of states is based on national interest" and "there exist permanent interests and those that reflect international circumstances." At the same time, he argued there was an important qualitative difference in the foreign policy of the Humala administration, noting its emphasis on investment, regional infrastructure, and educational and cultural exchange. Echoing the words of his predecessor, Foreign Minister García Belaúnde, Roncagliolo also argued that Humala's foreign policy was "free of ideological constraints that in the past motivated some unnecessary controversies with some of our neighbors" (Roncagliolo Orbegoso, interview with author, 20 October 2014).

Subregional, Regional, and International Relations

In a week-long tour of South America, President-elect Humala's first stop was Brazil where he met with President Dilma Vana Rousseff, reaffirming their strategic relationship. Over the next 12 months, Humala and Rousseff met three more times (Novak and Namihas 2012, 202–7). In November 2013, President Rousseff marked the end of the first decade of the strategic alliance with a state visit to Peru (*El Comercio*, 11 November 2013). In a tweet before her arrival, she noted that more than 70 Brazilian companies were now operating in Peru where they had invested US$6 billion, noting later that Peru ranked third in terms of Brazilian investments in South American states (MREP 2014, 29–30). Thereafter, President Humala maintained the momentum for increased integration with Brazil built up during the Toledo and García presidencies, strengthening old initiatives and introducing new ones (St John 2016, 154–55).

Most observers expected the Humala administration to be a strong supporter of UNASUR in part because of President Humala's close ties with Brazil, a prime mover behind its predecessor body. UNASUR was mentioned favorably in the program of progressive reform articulated by Humala in the 2006 presidential campaign, and Humala organized an extraordinary session of UNASUR in Lima shortly after his inauguration. Consequently, it came as a surprise when the Humala administration displayed a growing disinterest in regional integration in general and UNASUR in particular. Peru continued to play an active role in UNASUR, serving as president pro tempore from June 2012 to August 2013, but the focus of Peruvian foreign policy under Humala was elsewhere (MREP 2014, 45–46). The rationale behind this apparent shift in policy remained unstated; however, a reduced interest in South American integration was consistent with the Humala administration's emphasis on better relations with the United States and the Asia-Pacific Basin, notably APEC and the Pacific Alliance (Adins 2015, 252–53).

Launched by Brazil and Mexico in February 2010 and established in December 2011, the Comunidad de Estados Latinoamericanos y Caribenos (Community of Latin American and Caribbean States, CELAC) was the successor to the Rio Group and the Cumbre de América Latina y el Caribe (Latin American and Caribbean Summit, CALC). The agreement establishing CELAC incorporated political cooperation functions with inter-governmental coordination of public policies. Thereafter, CELAC emerged as a mechanism for dialogue focused on the coordination of efforts for cooperation, development, and integration (Novak and Namihas 2020, 201–3). With 33 member states, CELAC superimposed itself over subregional economic arrangements like CAN and MERCOSUR, regional coordinating bodies like UNASUR and ALBA, and international cooperation mechanisms like the OAS, ASPA, and the OEI. From the start, CELAC reflected strong ideological tensions among Latin American states with some members viewing it as a potential replacement for an OAS which they felt was dominated by the United States. In a body grounded in consensus, however, the majority of members continued to view CELAC as a valid and effective option but not a replacement for the OAS (Portales 2012; Segovia Hernández 2013).

To commemorate the 10th anniversary of the adoption of the Inter-American Democratic Charter, the Ministry of Foreign Affairs in September 2011 organized a symposium, "Diálogos sobre la Preservación y Promoción de la Democracia en las Américas" (Dialogues about the Preservation and Promotion of Democracy in the Americas). One year later, Foreign Minister Roncagliolo repeated calls made earlier by both the Toledo and García administrations in support of UN reforms, challenging the world body to better reflect the realities of the new millennium (Roncagliolo Orbegoso, interview with author, 20 October 2014). At the same time, Peruvian relations with the Middle East continued to expand with a state visit by the Emir of Qatar and the inauguration of Peruvian embassies in Saudi Arabia and Qatar and a consulate in Dubai (Sánchez Vargas de Ríos 2016, 11). In February 2016, President Recep Tayyip Erdogan of Turkey completed a state visit to Peru in which several new commercial, cooperation, and trade agreements were signed (Namihas 2016). Roncagliolo later stressed that wider relations with the Arab world did not imply an anti-Israeli stance, noting that President Humala in February 2014 visited Israel as well as Palestine and Qatar (Roncagliolo Orbegoso, interview with author, 20 October 2014). Peru also maintained its longtime support for UN peace-keeping missions (Sánchez 2014), and in December 2013, it launched its 22nd expedition to the Antarctic, continuing a policy dating back to the second Belaúnde administration (Belaúnde Terry, interview with author, 11 July 1983; Sánchez and Tielemans 2015).

During the Humala presidency, Peruvian involvement with the EU focused more on cooperation in multilateral forums, like the ICC and UNHRC, than on the negotiation of new bilateral agreements. A significant exception was a March 2016 agreement with the EU which enabled Peruvians to travel to the Schengen region for up to 90 days without a visa, a long-time foreign policy goal of Peru (*El Comercio*, 14 March 2016). Other areas of ongoing bilateral cooperation included sharing science and technology, enhancing security and defense, promoting arms control, strengthening human rights, and increasing commerce and trade (Novak and Namihas 2016, 109–48). Colombia, Peru, and the EU also signed a multilateral trade pact in Brussels in June 2012 (Sánchez Vargas de Ríos 2016, 10). Relations with individual EU member states remained positive with one exception. After Great Britain dispatched warships to the South Atlantic to mark the 30th anniversary of the Falklands/Malvinas War, Peru canceled a port visit by one of them to Lima's port of Callao, sparking a protest from the British government (Sánchez 2012).

Rapprochement

A long-time critic of the United States, Humala continued to criticize US policies throughout the 2011 presidential campaign; therefore, it came as a surprise when President Barack Obama reached out to him in the course of Humala's June 2011 informal visit to the White House. From that time forward, the Humala administration softened its tone toward the United States, expressing a desire to improve cooperation in areas like combating drug-related crime and terrorism. At the same time, it pursued increasingly friendly policies toward big businesses and multinational corporations (Renique 2013). During a June 2013 official visit to the White House, President Obama called Peru one of the "most reliable partners" in the hemisphere (*Bloomberg*, 11 June 2013), and President Humala described the Obama administration as "un socio con el cual se puede trabajar" (a partner with which one can work) (*El Comercio*, 11 June 2013). Reflecting the change in mood, the weekly news magazine *Caretas* titled its coverage of Humala's visit to the White House "El Nuevo Consenso" (The New Consensus) (*Caretas*, 13 June 2013). In November 2013, Foreign Minister Eva Rivas Franchini, who replaced Roncagliolo in May 2013, described relations with Washington as being at "un nivel muy alto" (a very high level) (*El Comercio*, 22 November 2013). In another welcomed development, Lori Berenson in December 2015 concluded her 20-year prison sentence and returned to the United States, ending a controversy that had bedeviled bilateral relations for more than two decades (*El Peruano*, 16 December 2016).

During the Humala government, diplomatic and commercial relations with the Russian Federation reached a level not seen since military governments ruled Peru in the *docenio* (1968–80). By the time Russian foreign minister Sergey Lavrov visited Peru in April 2014 to celebrate the 45th anniversary of the establishment of diplomatic relations, the Humala administration had purchased or was exploring the purchase of Russian fighter planes, tanks, and helicopters as part of President Humala's upgrade of the Peruvian armed forces (MREP 2014, 179). In so doing, the Humala government reaffirmed a policy of diversified arms transfers that dated back to the first Belaúnde administration (Cobas 1982, 152–59). In May 2014, Russian prime minister Dmitry Medvedev visited Peru, signing agreements on energy, hydrocarbons, scientific cooperation, and trade, and in November 2014, President Humala made a state visit to Russia, signing agreements on trade, climate protection, and tourism (*El Peruano*, 8 November 2014). On the sidelines of the November 2015 UN Conference on Climate Change in Paris, Presidents Humala and Vladimir Putin concluded a Joint Declaration of Strategic Partnership, the significance of which remained unclear (Novak and Namihas 2020, 212). Subsequent analysis suggested the pact was little more than a declarative statement contemplating the possibility of increased cooperation but not contributing in any concrete way to stronger bilateral ties. In any case, Peru continued to buy Russian aircraft, vehicles, and weapons, and hundreds of Peruvian students took advantage of Russian scholarships to study in the Russian Federation (Adins and Rooney 2019, 7).

A Quieter Neighborhood

The Humala administration was fully committed to the complete implementation of the 1998 Brasilia Accords. In a show of support for the settlement, President-elect Humala in June 2011 visited Ecuador to mark the UN registration of the Peru–Ecuador maritime treaty. Over the next five years, representatives of Peru and Ecuador met regularly in an ongoing effort to implement all aspects of the Brasilia Accords, including ongoing borderland development, improved border security, accelerated demining, and reduced transnational crime. In support of these goals, the governments of Ecuador and Peru in December 2015 created a 1.8-million-acre biosphere reserve on their shared border (MREP 2013, 26, 66–67; MREP 2014, 25–26, 31–33, 136–37, 162–64).

In the case of Colombia, bilateral relations continued to focus on defense and security issues as well as borderland development. In mid-2013, the two neighbors adopted a new plan to develop the frontier zone, the Plan de Desarrollo de la Zona de Integración Fronteriza Perú-Colombia, which concentrated on social, economic, and institutional projects. The plan was intended to strengthen the presence of the state in the frontier zone and to improve the quality of life of the people living there. In 2014, Colombia and Peru created a binational cabinet modeled on the one organized by Ecuador and Peru in 2007 to add focus to the many issues facing the borderland (MREP 2013, 29–30, 56; MREP 2014, 24, 31, 141, 159–60). At the second binational cabinet meeting in October 2015, talks between Presidents Humala and Juan Manuel Santos Calderón focused on defense, development, and security issues, concluding six new agreements (MREP 2015, 14–15; León Collazos 2016, 2, 4–5).

In October 2012, Peru and Bolivia concluded pacts intended to clarify disputed clauses of the October 2010 complementary protocol to the 1992 Ilo agreement. In February 2013, Bolivia, Brazil, and Peru also concluded a tripartite agreement to fight organized crime and drug trafficking in their frontier areas (MREP 2013, 28, 67–68; Novak and Namihas 2013, 233–36, 239–40). Even as the Ilo agreement continued to underperform, failing to meet Peruvian expectations of it as a platform to increase commercial interchange and to resolve long-standing issues of mutual interest, the Foreign Relations Committee of the Peruvian congress finally approved the pact in September 2013. The agreement still required ratification by the full congress before coming into effect; nevertheless, the Morales government touted the committee's decision and talked of the construction of a mega port near Ilo, together with a Bolivia–Brazil rail link (MREP 2014, 29, 164). In June 2015, the Bolivia–Peru binational cabinet met for the first time, and in July 2015, Peru and Bolivia concluded a strategic alliance consisting of more than 90 separate accords (MREP 2015, 14). In January 2016, Peru and Bolivia initiated a pact addressing the environmental restoration of Lake Titicaca (*La Razón*, 12 January 2016).

As early as 2009, the nationalist Humala questioned the approach taken by both the Toledo and García administrations to curb regional arms expenditures. He argued Peru should equip its armed forces on the basis of a clear doctrine of national defense and not as a function of what Chile or others were doing (*La República*, 4 May 2009). The Humala government signed the Arms Trade Treaty in September 2013 but also supported a major upgrade of the Peruvian armed forces.

President Humala also supported the decision of his predecessor to take the maritime dispute with Chile to the International Court of Justice at The Hague. Under the leadership of former foreign minister Allan Wagner, policy continuity on this issue eventually led to a favorable ICJ decision. In January 2014, the Court recognized Peruvian sovereignty over more than 50,000 km^2 of the Pacific Ocean, well over half the maritime space in

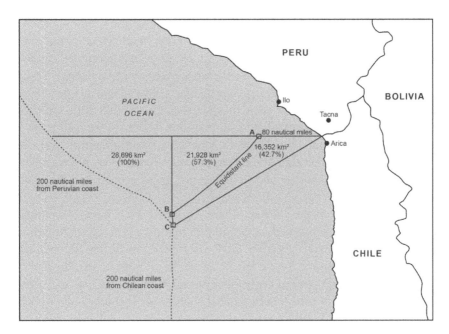

Figure 5.1 Decision of the International Court of Justice

Source: Nathan Bailey St John

dispute with Chile, including almost 22,000 km² of the disputed 38,000 km² in overlapping claims. On the other hand, Chile retained the bulk of the valuable coastal fishing grounds in the area (ICJ 2014, 55–67; Wieland Conroy 2017). Former foreign minister Roncagliolo proudly described the successful conclusion of the maritime dispute with Chile "as a process of delimitation of Peruvian territory that started with our national independence" (Roncagliolo Orbegoso, interview with author, 20 October 2014). In an address to the Peruvian Diplomatic Academy, Ambassador Ana María Liliana Sánchez Vargas de Ríos, the foreign minister of Peru for the final 16 months of the Humala presidency, praised the final resolution of the Chile-Peru maritime dispute. *Este triunfo representa el mayor logro de la política exterior de este gobierno* (This triumph represents the major success of the foreign policy of this government) (Sánchez Vargas de Ríos 2016, 15–17, quote 16).

Focus Asia

During the Humala administration, Peru continued to pursue trade agreements around the world; however, its approach here was more an affirmation of the policies of the Toledo and García administrations than any real departure from them (MREP 2013, 43–44, 73, 85–87; MREP 2014, 38–43, 81–84, 144–54, 210–18). The free trade agreement with South Korea, concluded at the end of the García administration, took effect in August 2011, and in November 2011, Peru concluded a new air services agreement with South Korea. In March 2012, the free trade agreement with Japan which was negotiated by the García administration came into effect, and in October 2013, Peru and Japan celebrated 140 years of diplomatic relations. After the Peruvian congress in December 2012 approved the Peru–Colombia trade agreement with the EU signed by the Humala administration earlier in the year, it meant Peru now had similar trade agreements with every major economy in the world (Stevens et al. 2012).

At the creation of the Pacific Alliance in April 2011, Chile, Colombia, Mexico, and Peru accounted for around 36 percent of the Latin American population, and their collective GDP made the newly created alliance the eighth most important economy in the world. In its first year, the Pacific Alliance received 41 percent of the investments in the region and accounted for 50 percent of Latin American and Caribbean exports and imports. Moreover, average GDP growth rates for some Pacific Alliance countries were higher than those for ALBA or MERCOSUR. In part for these reasons, members of the Latin American left were critical of the Pacific Alliance, viewing it as an instrument of US hegemony intended to subvert regional integration and promote US views on trade issues. In contrast, Brazil downplayed the significance of the Pacific Alliance even though it clearly affected its regional power projection as well as impacting on the regional integration and cooperative dynamics of both ALBA and MERCOSUR (Nolte and Wehner 2013, 1, 3, 6). Undeterred, the member states of the Pacific Alliance continued their efforts to integrate free markets in trade, energy, and infrastructure, agreeing in February 2014 to an additional protocol removing tariffs on 92 percent of goods and services (Fuentes Cervantes 2018, 44–45; Novak and Namihas 2020, 198–201). In February 2016, Peru joined 11 other Pacific Rim states, including Chile and Mexico, in signing the controversial Trans-Pacific Partnership (TPP), the largest regional trade accord in history (Sánchez Vargas de Ríos 2016, 9–10; Novak and Namihas 2018a, 28–29, 71–121, 130–31).

When Presidents Humala and Hu Jintao met at the November 2011 APEC meeting in Honolulu, they pledged to work together to advance the strategic partnership formed in 2008. One year later, bilateral trade between China and Peru had more than doubled since the free trade agreement took effect in 2010, and China surpassed the United States as Peru's main trading partner (*Merco Press*, 30 November 2011; Flannery 2013). In February 2013, Foreign Minister Roncagliolo visited China where he announced that China would quadruple the number of scholarships available to Peruvian students to study in China, especially in science and technology (Zanabria 2015, 90–91). In April 2013, President Humala visited China, met with newly-elected President Xi Jinping, and promoted Peruvian exports and Chinese investment in Peru (MREP 2013, 36, 82). With commercial ties the main driver of the bilateral relationship, the strategic partnership was elevated to a comprehensive strategic partnership in 2013. In May 2015, Chinese Premier Li Keqiang visited Lima to promote the comprehensive strategic partnership and to conclude 10 new bilateral pacts (*El Peruano*, 23 May 2015), and in December 2015, a Chinese naval hospital ship paid a seven-day service call at Lima's port of Callao. This was the vessel's first-ever stop at a South American port, and the port call was viewed as a fresh sign of China's growing influence in the region (*Associated Press*, 22 December 2015).

A central element of the Peruvian approach to China during the Humala administration was the concept of Peru as a regional hub in South America. Motivated in part by a desire to reduce shipping costs and avoid the Panama Canal, China supported the Peruvian vision of being a gateway to the Pacific (Fuentes Cervantes 2018, 44). The Chinese government also supported the proposed construction of an Amazonian railway linking the Atlantic coast of Brazil to the Pacific coast of Peru (*El Comercio*, 23 May 2015). Nevertheless, the project remained controversial with the government of President Pedro Pablo Kuczynski later suggesting it might be too expensive and environmentally harmful to build (Alden and Méndez 2019, 278).

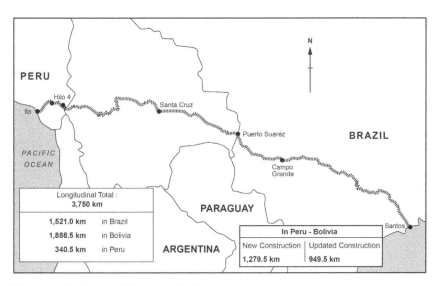

Figure 5.2 Proposed Bioceanic Railway

Source: Nathan Bailey St John

Anti-mining protests led by indigenous groups and rural residents tested China-Peru ties in this period. Opposition to large-scale mining projects did not necessarily reflect hostility to China in particular. Instead, the mobilizations often were based on ancestral claims, indigenous rights, water scarcity, environmental concerns, and the distribution of mining rents (Renique 2013).

Conclusions

For the most part, the foreign policy of the Humala administration was an affirmation of the foreign policies of the Toledo and García governments as opposed to any meaningful departure from them. Peru remained an active participant in a number of subregional, regional, and international bodies, expanded its strategic relationship with Brazil, and continued to cooperate with neighboring states, like Bolivia, Colombia, and Ecuador. Ties with the United States improved, notably in areas of shared policy concerns like drug-related crime and terrorism. The People's Republic of China and the Russian Federation were the two areas where the most significant changes occurred. Peru's strategic relationship with China broadened and deepened with the latter surpassing the United States as Peru's main trading partner. Commercial and diplomatic relations with Russia also increased, reaching a level not seen in more than 30 years. Finally, the ICJ in 2014 issued a ruling on the maritime boundary dispute with Chile largely to Peru's advantage in a legal case initiated by President García and successfully concluded by President Humala.

Chapter 6

PEDRO-PABLO KUCZYNSKI GODARD TO FRANCISCO RAFAEL SAGASTI HOCHHAUSLER, 2016–2021

Throughout most of the 2016 presidential campaign, Keiko Fujimori was the front runner with Pedro-Pablo Kuczynski Godard, a wealthy investment banker with considerable international financial experience, occupying third or fourth place in most polls. Kuczynski was well known in Peruvian political circles, having served as an economic adviser and manager of the central bank during the first Belaúnde Terry administration and both finance minister and prime minister in the Toledo administration. Kuczynski's prospects improved in March when the candidates polling in second and fourth place were disqualified. Fujimori won the first round with 39.82 percent of the vote with Kuczynski in second place with 20.98 percent (Horler and Cazarez 2016). In the second round, Kuczynski benefitted from the endorsement of the leftist politician Verónika Mendoza, who placed third in the first round, and a strong anti-*fujimorista* animus among the electorate. Kuczynski won the second round by the narrow margin of 42,597 votes (Crabtree and Durand 2017, 186).

Rise and Fall of Kuczynski

On 28 July 2016, President Kuczynski appointed Víctor Ricardo Luna Mendoza, a career diplomat who had served as ambassador to the United States (1992–99) and Great Britain (2006–2010), as minister of foreign affairs. In a succinct overview of Peruvian foreign policy, Ambassador Luna highlighted the key components of the foreign policy of the Kuczynski administration. With neighboring Bolivia, Brazil, Chile, Colombia, and Ecuador, he planned to continue binational cabinet meetings in conjunction with targeted programs for each country with the intent to encourage development in the borderlands. On the regional level, he prioritized the Pacific Alliance, noting blocs like ALBA, CAN, CELAC, and UNASUR often were competitive instead of complementary in their promotion of integration and development. Elsewhere, Luna recognized the need for institutional change at the United Nations, arguing the best way to effect change was for Peru to take a leadership role. As a former ambassador to the United States, he also recognized the importance of maintaining good relationships with the White House even as Peru continued to expand its ties with China and the European Union. Finally, Luna promised to better serve Peruvians abroad by continuing efforts to improve efficiency and reduce bureaucracy at Peruvian embassies and consulates (Luna Mendoza 2016).

In his inaugural address, President Kuczynski focused on his domestic agenda, highlighting education, health care, and infrastructure as some of the areas his government would emphasize. In the process, he pledged to pursue a social revolution that would lead to a more modern, equitable, and supportive Peru. His discussion of foreign policy was limited to two short paragraphs at the end of his address in which he promised Peruvian leadership in regional cooperation and integration as well as more attention to the well being of Peruvians in the borderlands. He also promised Peru would become a member of the Organization for Economic Cooperation and Development (OECD) by 2021 (Kuczynski 2016).

President Kuczynski inherited a Peru in which macroeconomic growth rates were high but trust in democratic institutions was low with crime and citizen security at the top of voter concerns. Early policy initiatives by the Kuczynski administration, notably support for mining in the region of Junín, an initiative to relax environmental standards, and a call to extend the deadline for closing the smelter at La Oroya were heavily criticized by all sides in congress. Kuczynski's abortive attempt to form a legislative alliance with Keiko Fujimori's center-right Fuerza Popular (FP) party after Verónika Mendoza's support had proved decisive in his second round election further aggravated the political left in congress (Valladares 2016). At the same time, the foreign policy of the Kuczynski administration under the leadership of Foreign Minister Luna was widely popular, receiving high marks in early public opinion polls (*La República*, 20 July 2017).

Threaten with impeachment by the opposition controlled legislature, President Kuczynski on Christmas Eve 2017 pardoned former president Alberto Fujimori, serving a 25-year prison term for corruption and human rights violations. In return, a faction of the FP party led by Keiko Fujimori's brother, Kenji, agreed to abstain in an impeachment motion, denying the opposition the supermajority needed to remove him (*New York Times*, 24 December 2017). When fresh accusations of corruption and wrongdoing surfaced, Kuczynski found himself politically isolated, and in March 2018, he was forced to resign (Cameron 2019, 104).

Martín Alberto Vizcarra Cornejo (23 March 2018 to 10 November 2020)

With the resignation of Kuczynski, Martín Alberto Vizcarra Cornejo, the first vice president, assumed the presidency (*El Peruano*, 3 April 2018). An engineer, former governor of the department of Moquegua, and former ambassador to Canada, he had never aspired to the presidency (Goodman 2018, 4–5). During his first year in office, the opposition-controlled congress, a body in which more than half its members faced investigations for corruption, disrupted his legislative agenda which largely focused on anti-corruption and anti-impunity reforms. Recognizing the electorate had grown tired of partisan bickering and endless corruption scandals, President Vizcarra in September 2019 took a page out of former president Fujimori's playbook, dissolving congress and calling for legislative elections in January 2020 (Toledo Orozco 2019).

The advent of the novel coronavirus (COVID-19) shortly after the January 2020 elections exposed deep socioeconomic problems in Peru, confronting it with a health care crisis of historic proportions. Early on, President Vizcarra won high marks for his decisive response to the pandemic, quickly implementing one of the region's most stringent lockdowns, but as time passed, his administration found it difficult to contain the virus and to return to normal levels of economic activity. Despite stay-at-home orders, curfews, and border closings, poverty and overcrowding resulted in Peru for a time having the highest per capita death rate in the world (*New York Times*, 20 June 2020).

In November 2020, congress removed the popular Vizcarra from office on the controversial grounds of permanent moral incapacity, a provision in the 1993 constitution that allowed the impeachment of former president Fujimori (*La República*, 9 November 2020). Several factors contributed to Vizcarra's downfall, including resistance to his anti-corruption reforms, the absence of stable, institutional political parties, and a unicameral legislature in which checks and balances were fragile (Dunkelberg 2020). With the post of vice president vacant, Manuel Arturo Merino de Lama, speaker of the congress and architect of Vizcarra's downfall, replaced him as president on 10 November 2020. Faced with an unprecedented public outcry after demonstrations left two dead and dozens injured, Merino stepped down after five days in office.

Francisco Rafael Sagasti Hochhausler (15 November 2020 to 28 July 2021)

Congress replaced Merino with Francisco Rafael Sagasti Hochhausler, a centrist lawmaker. The third president in a week, Sagasti's primary duty was to ensure fair and transparent elections in April 2021 (*El Peruano*,

18 November 2020). In his inaugural address, he quoted a passage from a poem by the beloved Peruvian poet, César Vallejo, highlighting Sagasti's belief that uniting the country was his most important job (Eshleman 2007, 404–5). In the office, President Sagasti faced a severe political crisis, raging pandemic, and deep economic recession, challenges that demanded extensive reforms impossible for an interim head of state to implement (Burt 2020).

Subregional, Regional, and International Integration

In August 2016, the Peruvian congress adopted a declaration calling on Venezuelan president Nicolás Maduro to release political prisoners and to respect a recall vote. In March 2017, the Maduro government labeled President Kuczynski a "coward" and a "dog," and in response, the Kuczynski government recalled its ambassador to Venezuela (*Reuters*, 6 March 2017). Later in the month, Peru supported an OAS resolution calling on Venezuela to negotiate an end to the crisis arising from food and medical shortages. In August 2017, Foreign Minister Luna hosted a meeting of Latin American foreign ministers to discuss the Venezuelan emergency (Luna Mendoza 2022). Peru's expressed concern at the time was a growing humanitarian crisis that had sent waves of refugees to adjoining states. In a major diplomatic achievement for Peruvian foreign policy in general and Foreign Minister Luna in particular, Peru at the end of the meeting joined 10 other Latin American countries plus Canada in signing the Declaración de Lima (Lima Declaration). Condemning the rupture of the democratic order in Venezuela, the declaration established the Lima Group, a multilateral effort to find a peaceful resolution to the Venezuelan crisis (*Caretas*, 10 August 2017).

Events in Venezuela produced one of the largest displacements of people in recent times with more than four million Venezuelans fleeing their home country. By 2020, Peru was hosting more than one million Venezuelans, second only to Colombia. Initially, the Kuczynski government welcomed the refugees; however, as their numbers swelled, they provoked a backlash in Peru (Ble, Leghtas, and Graham 2020). Néstor Popolizio Bardales, foreign minister for the first 18 months of the Vizcarra administration, addressed the issue in a 2019 interview. "The impact of this massive migration has been significant in the domestic labor market, as well as in our health and education systems. It is clear that our institutional capabilities have been overwhelmed...." (Popolizio Bardales 2019). In response, the Vizcarra government tried to strike more of a balance by integrating some Venezuelans into Peruvian society while signaling to Peruvians that it understood their growing fatigue (Popolizio Bardales 2022). Following changes to visa regulations, net levels of migration had fallen to zero by mid-2019 (Winter 2020).

In early January 2019, Peru joined other members of the Lima Group in refusing to recognize Maduro's mandate for a second term. Shortly thereafter, the Vizcarra administration withdrew its charge d'affaires in Caracas and recognized Venezuelan opposition leader Juan Guaidó as Venezuela's interim president (*Caretas*, 21 February 2019). At the same time, the Lima Group stated they were opposed to a military intervention to end the crisis in Venezuela, opening an apparent breach with the United States which maintained all options were on the table. In early 2020, the Vizcarra administration joined other Lima Group members in backing the reelection of Guaidó as head of the Venezuelan congress after the Maduro government forced a separate vote imposing a new congressional leader (*Reuters*, 6 January 2020).

Over time, political change throughout the region, compounded by the absence of supranational institutions, lax organization design, and the preeminence of national autonomy, undermined the viability of UNASUR. Argentina, Brazil, Chile, Paraguay, and Peru suspended participation in April 2018, and Colombia withdrew in August of that year (Bilotta 2018, 11). On 22 March 2019, Argentina, Brazil, Colombia, Chile, Ecuador, Guyana, Paraguay, and Peru signed the Declaración de Santiago (Santiago Declaration), creating a new regional bloc, the Foro para el Progreso y Integración de América Latina (Forum for the Progress and Integration of South America, PROSUR). The Santiago Declaration restricted PROSUR membership to states with the "full enjoyment of democracy" (*New York Times en español*, 29 March 2019).

In April 2017, the Kuczynski administration participated in the inaugural meeting of the Ancient Civilizations Forum in Athens, Greece. Bolivia, China, Egypt, Greece, Italy, Iran, Iraq, and Peru, with the addition of Armenia, formed a cultural initiative among countries that considered themselves to be cradles of civilization. The Ancient Civilizations Forum aimed "to transform culture into a source of soft power and a fundamental tool of modern and multidimensional foreign policy." It also hoped "to highlight international cultural cooperation as a factor for economic development" (Ancient Civilizations Forum 2017). The immediate focus of the Forum was on cultural issues, but Foreign Minister Luna thought it might eventually widened its concerns to include diplomatic and political issues (Luna Mendoza 2022).

In June 2017, the 47th OAS General Assembly meeting in Cancun, Mexico adopted a Peruvian proposal highlighting corruption as a systemic threat to the Western Hemisphere (OAS 2017). As a result, Democratic Governance against Corruption was the theme of the Eighth Summit of the Americas held in Lima in April 2018 (Luna Mendoza 2022). President Vizcarra termed the summit a success, but some observers considered it a lost opportunity (Stuenkel 2018). President Donald J. Trump, facing legal troubles at home and a crisis in Syria abroad, canceled at the last moment, becoming the first US president not to attend a Summit of the Americas, and Peru disinvited Venezuelan president Nicolás Maduro. The Compromiso de Lima (Lima Commitment), adopted at the end of the summit, called on participants to take concrete actions to strengthen democratic institutions in the fight against corruption (OAS 2018; Popolizio Bardales 2022). With Brazilian construction giant Odebrecht at the heart of corruption scandals across the region and some attendees facing corruption allegations at home, the summit's emphasis on corruption was ironic. The summit also highlighted an inter-American system in need of reform and the contradictory strains wracking US policy toward the Americas (Erikson 2018).

On 24 July 2018, representatives of the member states of the Pacific Alliance and MERCOSUR met in Puerto Vallarta, Mexico, and signed a joint declaration intended to strengthen commercial, economic, and social ties. At the time, the two blocs represented approximately 81 percent of the region's population and 86 percent of its GDP. They also represented 89 percent of exports and 88 percent of inflows of FDI to Latin America and the Caribbean. The joint declaration was the culmination of work begun in 2014 to identify cooperative actions that might lead eventually to a trade agreement between them (Palacio 2020).

In the closing days of the Kuczynski administration, Peru joined other Latin American and Caribbean states in agreeing to the Escazú Accord, a regional agreement covering access to public information, public participation, and justice in environmental matters (*La República*, 13 August 2022). On 6 September 2019, President Vizcarra joined the heads of state of Bolivia, Colombia, and Ecuador, together with representatives from Brazil, Guyana, and Suriname, to sign a landmark agreement intended to protect the Amazon rainforest. The Pacto de Leticia (Leticia Pact) aimed to drive sustainable forest use and reforestation, restore degraded land, improve information sharing on deforestation and wildfires, and empower indigenous groups (MREP 2019b). From the start, the Leticia Pact was criticized as little more than a photo op that lacked scientific detail, enforcement mechanisms, and funding. Two years later, the pledges in the Leticia Pact remained largely unfilled due to political differences, conflicting economic motivations, and COVID-19 distractions (*Reuters*, 21 October 2021).

Borderland Developments

Diplomacy with neighboring states reflected the desire of successive Peruvian governments, including the Kuczynski, Vizcarra, and Sagasti administrations, to safeguard their citizens, especially those living in the borderlands (Novak and Namihas 2020, 205–7, 234–37). In so doing, Peru depended increasingly on the binational cabinet forum first established with Ecuador in 2007 (Luna Mendoza 2017; León Collazos 2018, 2). During the second Bolivia–Peru binational cabinet meeting in November 2016, Presidents Kuczynski and Evo Morales signed the Declaración de Sucre (Sucre Declaration), addressing common issues like cross boundary water resources, transnational crime, and the rights of women and children (*La Razón*, 4 November 2016; MREP 2017, 13). At the fourth binational cabinet meeting held in September 2018, Peru and Bolivia concluded an additional 180 commitments, covering security and defense, economic development, infrastructure integration, and related borderland issues (MREP 2019a, 10).

On 29 November 2016, President Kuczynski met with Chilean president Michelle Bachelet Jeria and agreed to begin binational cabinet meetings in June 2017 (MREP 2017, 13; Luna Mendoza 2022). Former foreign minister Eduardo Ferrero Costa was one among many Peruvians who supported this initiative, noting that past Peruvian experience with binational cabinet meetings with Bolivia, Colombia, and Ecuador "had been positive" (*El Comercio*, 28 November 2016). In their second binational cabinet meeting in November 2018, President Vizcarra and his Chilean counterpart, President Sebastían Piñera signed 14 accords and 133 lines of action, addressing five themes: social and cultural affairs; security and defense; foreign trade, investments, and tourism; energy, mining, environment, and sustainable development; infrastructure; and frontier integration (*Caretas*, 29 November 2018; MREP 2019a, 10). At their third binational cabinet meeting in October 2019, Presidents Vizcarra and Piñera focused on improving health care and reducing gender based violence in the borderlands (*La República*, 10 October 2019).

At the 10th Ecuador–Peru binational cabinet meeting in October 2016, Presidents Kuczynski and Rafael Correa reaffirmed their mutual intent to construct a common future (MREP 2017, 12–13). In June 2017, the Kuczynski administration urged the Correa government to halt the construction of a wall along the border intended by Ecuador to stop smuggling and help control flooding. In addition to violating the 1998 Brasilia Accords, Peru argued the wall would disrupt cross border integration and disturb the flow of water in a canal separating the two countries, increasing flood risks in Peru (*Reuters*, 6 June 2017). After Peru recalled its ambassador to Ecuador in protest, President Lenín Moreno agreed to suspend construction of the wall, pending further discussions (*Reuters*, 13 July 2017). At the 11th binational cabinet meeting, Presidents Kuczynski and Moreno signed the Declaración de Trujillo (Trujillo Declaration), reaffirming their commitment to work together to integrate their peoples (*Andina*, 20 October 2017). In October 2018, President

Vizcarra traveled to Quito to meet with President Moreno and to celebrate the 20th anniversary of the signing of the 1998 peace agreements (MREP 2019a, 10).

By the end of the third Colombia–Peru binational cabinet meeting, which took place in late January 2017, Colombia and Peru had adopted more than 300 bilateral agreements since the first meeting in 2014, a testimony to bilateral cooperation and the binational cabinet meeting format (León Collazos 2018, 4–5). Dialogue at the fourth binational cabinet meeting in February 2018 centered on five themes: security and defense; trade, economic development, and tourism; environment, energy, and mining; social affairs and governance; and migration and border issues. The meeting led to the conclusion of more than 130 commitments and 12 agreements, including the commencement of the Border Integration Zone Development Fund, an initiative to execute binational projects for vulnerable populations (MREP 2019a, 10).

China

Every Peruvian president in the twenty-first century prioritized wider relations with China, exchanging official visits and concluding multiple agreements. President Kuczynski continued this policy, signaling the importance of China to Peru by choosing China as the destination for his first trip abroad (Alden and Méndez 2019, 293). During his visit, he emphasized investment and trade, and at its end, he noted how grateful Chinese authorities were that China was his first destination (Ramírez Bullón and Ayala Castiblanco 2017, 24). Two months later, President Xi Jinping participated in the APEC forum in Lima, extending his stay to conclude 18 new agreements. Alluding to the protectionist policies of the Trump administration, the Chinese leader also reaffirmed his commitment to free markets (Cardenal 2017, 81–82). In early February 2017, the Kuczynski government defended China as a good trade partner after US Secretary of State Rex Tillerson warned Latin American nations against excessive reliance on economic ties with China. In May 2019, Peru joined China's Belt and Road Initiative (BRI), and a few days later, President Vizcarra announced that new project studies suggested Bolivia and Peru might still partner with China to build the Bioceanic Railway (*Reuters*, 12 May 2019).

Even as the number of agreements linking Peru and China grew, some Peruvian academics and diplomats criticized the lack of progress in creating a comprehensive vision and integrated strategy for China (Zanabria 2015, 94–95; Ramírez Bullón and Ayala Castiblanco 2017, 24–26). The Chinese style of business, especially its disregard for environmental issues and aggressive exploitation of marine resources, also drew criticism, highlighting the recurrent nexus between domestic and foreign policy in Peru. The pollution of local water supplies and perceived lack of support for local communities by Chinese and US mining companies in regions like Ancash and Cajamarca, as well as the Chinese-owned iron ore mine in Ica and the Las Bambas copper mine in Apurimac, continued to spark protests during the Kuczynski, Vizcarra, and Sagasti governments (*Reuters*, 27 October 2021).

Russia

In February 2019, Peru and the Russian Federation celebrated the 50th anniversary of their establishment of diplomatic relations. By that time, intergovernmental bodies had been established to address military, commercial, scientific, and technical cooperation, together with political consultations and fishing issues (Adins and Rooney 2019, 6; Novak and Namihas 2020, 211–12). The foreign policy of the Kuczynski administration focused on relations with the United States, entry into the OECD, the Pacific Alliance, APEC, and China. Russian relations also were not a priority for the Vizcarra government which was more concerned with Andean affairs, Venezuela, Peru as a non-permanent member of the UN Security Council, the United States, and China (Adins and Rooney 2019, 160–62). Consequently, bilateral trade between Peru and Russia remained at a relatively low level, characterized by a systematic deficit for Peru, and Russian investment in Peru was negligible. In the end, the Peru–Russia relationship was mostly confined to the purchase of Soviet weaponry and the technical cooperation necessary to upgrade and repower Soviet military equipment already in the Peruvian inventory (Cardenal 2017, 83–84; Adins and Rooney 2019, 6–8).

United States

President Kuczynski's background and promotion of market oriented policies earned him the immediate support of the Barack Obama administration. President Obama attended the APEC summit in Lima in November 2016 where he met with Kuczynski (MREP 2017, 14). President Kuczynski also shared some viewpoints with President Donald J. Trump, notably on Venezuela and Nicaragua. That said, when Kuczynski in February 2017 met Trump in the White House, the first Latin American chief executive to do so, policy differences quickly surfaced. On trade, Kuczynski emphasized the need to deepen trade agreements as evidenced by Peruvian participation in the Trans-Pacific Partnership (TPP). After the Trump administration withdrew from TPP on 20 January 2017, Peru joined 10 other countries in forming the Comprehensive and Progressive Agreement for

Trans-Pacific Partnership (CPTPP), better known as TPP-11, on 8 March 2018 (Novak and Namihas 2018b, 93, 103). After his February 2017 meeting with Trump, Kuczynski declined to comment specifically on Trump's proposal to build a wall between Mexico and the United States, but he told the media that he preferred bridges to walls and favored the free movement of people across borders (*Reuters*, 24 February 2017). Other policy areas where the Kuczynski, Vizcarra, and Sagasti governments clearly disagreed with the Trump administration included but were not limited to climate change, democratic governance, and the environment.

In the end, the Trump administration mostly ignored Latin America as part of a broader strategy of withdrawal from international affairs (Novak and Namihas 2018b, 87–115). In contrast, the Joseph R. Biden, Jr. administration, inaugurated during the Sagasti caretaker government, promised the region in general and Peru in particular increased attention, structure, and certainty. Serving as vice president under President Obama, Biden made 16 trips to Latin America, more than any other US president or vice president in US history (Paz 2020). President-elect Biden pledged to end the incompetence and neglect that characterized Trump's approach to Latin America and the Caribbean and to restore US hemispheric leadership based on the principles of respect, responsibility, and partnership (Camilleri 2020). In a virtual conference after Biden's inauguration, President Sagasti indicated that he expected Peruvian relations with the United States to improve during the Biden administration, citing the economy, climate change, narco-trafficking, and organized crime as areas of mutual concern (*El Peruano*, 18 February 2021).

Finally, President Kuczynski in June 2017 visited France, meeting with President Emmanuel Macron and urging French entrepreneurs to invest in Peru (*Andina*, 11 June 2017). In March 2021, President Sagasti announced that Peru would team with France to construct a new central highway. This US$3.1 billion project would unite the central region of Peru with the central coast (*El Peruano*, 24 March 2021).

Conclusions

Between July 2016 and July 2021, Peru had four presidents and eight foreign ministers. Personalist political parties, weak institutions, and a fractured congress added to the chaos and uncertainty, making it difficult to achieve policy continuity let alone policy innovation in either domestic or foreign policy. Moreover, the final 18 months of this period were dominated by a global pandemic whose severity overwhelmed the human and financial resources of the state. The pandemic also restricted global mobility, resulting in the cancellation or postponement of many international conferences, gatherings, and meetings. At the same time, the contagion accelerated preexisting tendencies within the international community and drew attention to contradictions in the international system. In this unfamiliar and uncertain milieu, foreign policy initiatives by Peru and most other states were relatively limited in number and significance with a few exceptions like the creation of the Lima Group, the Lima Commitment to fight corruption, and the creation of PROSUR; consequently, the foreign policy of Peru for much of this period was largely one of maintenance as opposed to fresh steps in new directions.

Chapter 7

JOSÉ PEDRO CASTILLO TERRONES TO DINA ERCILIA BOLUARTE ZEGARRA, 2021–2023

Following a period of extended political instability, an unprecedented 18 candidates sought the presidency in April 2021. When the ballots were tabulated, José Pedro Castillo Terrones, a school teacher, union leader, and self-proclaimed Marxist-Leninist, was the surprise winner in the first round with 18.99 percent of the vote, and Keiko Fujimori was in second place with 13.39 percent (*El Comercio*, 20 April 2021). Castillo won the second round with 50.13 percent of valid votes due to overwhelming support in the poorest areas of the country and in key mining regions, like Cotabambas, Espinar, and Chumbivilcas (*El Comercio*, 16 June 2021). Keiko Fujimori, who finished second for the third time, cried foul without evidence to back up claims of fraud, and once she exhausted every avenue to substantiate them, Castillo was declared the winner.

During the campaign, Castillo promised to rewrite the constitution, spend 10 percent of the GDP on education and health care, restructure the pension system and nationalize the energy industry (*La República*, 18 April 2021). His socialist platform alarmed international investors and the political class of Peru who feared his administration would end the free market economic model in place since the early years of the Fujimori government. Castillo responded to his critics by softening earlier proposals, promising a technocratic heavy cabinet and moderate economic policies. These changes temporarily calmed nervous investors and financial markets; nevertheless, his election was expected to lead to an extended period of political unrest. Of 130 congressional seats, Perú Libre, the party that nominated Castillo for the presidency, won only 37; consequently, Castillo was forced to govern without a congressional majority. Keiko Fujimori's Fuerza Popular party took 24 seats, presenting a small but determined opposition (Moncada 2021).

Democracy in Peru

The election of Pedro Castillo highlighted the many problems undermining democracy in Peru. Low levels of institutional legitimacy, a weak party system, an often corrupt unicameral legislature, and the repeat appearance of outsiders in the political arena have plagued Peru for three decades (Paz-Soldan 2022). The ongoing conflict between the executive and legislative branches of government was the most persistent problem as it made it difficult if not impossible for chief executives to enact the policies, they promised during their election campaigns (Shifter 2021). In addition, President Castillo's inner circle from the start faced a growing chorus of serious allegations of mismanagement and corruption, and the pandemic remained a challenge for Peru which continued to suffer high rates of infection (Martínez 2022).

For a time, the economy proved to be the one bright spot, largely due to experienced and pragmatic leadership at the finance ministry (IMF 2022, 4–9). In an impressive recovery from a double-digit recession in 2020, Peru's GDP grew by 13.5 percent in 2021 (*El Peruano*, 1 February 2022). At the same time, Peru continued to rely mostly on mining and petroleum revenues while the other economic issues that candidate Castillo promised to address, like low wages and high levels of labor informality, continued to restrain growth and development (Sweigart 2022). As citizen mobilizations increased in response to unfulfilled campaign promises, the president's approval rating dropped to 20 percent in mid-July 2022. In the second year of the Castillo presidency, an increasingly disruptive political crisis, combative congress, and global economic pressures combined to lower economic growth expectations (*Reuters*, 18 August 2022).

Continuity in Foreign Policy

Castillo appointed Héctor Béjar Rivera, an 85-year-old veteran of the 1960s guerrilla movements, as minister of foreign affairs (Béjar Rivera 1969). In a 2 August 2018 address marking his appointment, Béjar outlined an agenda that suggested substantial change in the direction of Peruvian foreign policy. Among other things, he said the Castillo government would retire from congressional consideration the file which asked congress to approve Peru's withdrawal from UNASUR, announced Peru's intent to strengthen CELAC, and implied Peru would withdraw from the Lima Group (MREP 2021a). Handicapped by a long history of controversial statements, Béjar was forced to resign after only 18 days in office (*La República*, 17 August 2021).

To replace him, Castillo appointed Óscar Maúrtua de Romaña, secretary general to President Fernando Belaúnde Terry during his second term and foreign minister in the last year of the Toledo administration (Maúrtua de Romaña, interviews with author, 11 July 1983, 18 April 2006). The appointment of Maúrtua, a career diplomat, was widely applauded by Peru's political class but spurred discontent within Perú Libre which argued the viewpoints of Maúrtua did not express the sentiment of a radical leftist party (*La República*, 21 August 2021). Days later, the Castillo administration appointed Ambassador Manuel Rodríguez Cuadros, vice minister or minister of foreign affairs for 50 of the 60 months of the Toledo government, as Peru's UN representative, an appointment also criticized by Perú Libre (*El Peruano*, 31 August 2021).

Under the leadership of Foreign Minister Maúrtua, the Ministry of Foreign Affairs was a stabilizing force in the early months of the Castillo administration. It focused on the traditional concerns of Peruvian foreign policy in initiatives that reflected continuity and balance at a time when many Peruvians favored some change in domestic policy but opposed any radical shift in foreign policy. Maúrtua assigned maximum importance to obtaining an adequate supply of COVID-19 vaccines, prioritized regular binational meetings with neighboring states, and encouraged regional integration through UNASUR, MERCOSUR, and CELAC. He also promoted foreign investment in international forums from Davos to the UN, reaffirmed Peru's active participation in the Pacific Alliance, pursued membership in OECD, and exhorted consuls to improve their services to Peruvians abroad (MREP 2021b).

Signaling the importance of the China-Peru relationship, President-elect Castillo chose the Chinese embassy as his first embassy visit. In August 2021, Peru's energy and mining minister also reached out to the heads of some of the largest Chinese mining companies in Peru; nevertheless, these operations remained the target of social protests in the coming months (Sweigart and Cohen 2021). In November 2021, China and Peru commemorated the 50th anniversary of their establishment of diplomatic relations. At the time, President Castillo emphasized that China was Peru's "main trading partner" and that ties between the two countries had strengthened "since we upgraded our relationship to a comprehensive strategic partnership" (*El Peruano*, 1 November 2021). According to the Peruvian ambassador to China, Luis Quesada, Peru at the time was the second largest destination for Chinese investment in Latin America, and it was one of only three countries in the region to have free trade agreements with China (Lo Lau 2022, 2). In the future, China will remain an important trading partner for Peru. That said, the 20th National Congress of the Chinese Communist Party, meeting in Beijing in October 2022, confirmed Chinese expectations that their rate of economic growth will slow over time. Slower economic growth will affect Latin American economies like Peru in important ways.

It will reduce direct demand for Latin American exports, act as a drag on commodity prices, and decrease Chinese investment throughout the region (Larraín and Zhang 2023).

In mid-September, Castillo traveled to Mexico to attend the sixth CELAC summit where informal discussions among participants included the possibility of CELAC replacing the OAS (*Reuters*, 17 September 2021). At the meeting, Castillo delivered an impassioned address in which he called for Latin American and Caribbean unity and integration but stopped short of endorsing the replacement of the OAS with CELAC. Instead, he called for CELAC to focus on the pandemic, terrorism, organized crime, and corruption (*El Peruano*, 18 September 2021).

From Mexico City, President Castillo flew to Washington, DC, and then on to New York. Throughout his visit to the United States, he affirmed his commitment to democracy and human rights as part of an effort to reassure international financiers and encourage investment in Peru (*Miami Herald*, 25 September 2021). Thereafter, US policy toward Peru remained friendly albeit restrained in tone and somewhat limited in scope as Washington watched to see if Castillo would walk the talk when it came to democracy, human rights, and expropriation. When Undersecretary of State Wendy Sherman visited Lima in early November 2021, talks with President Castillo and Foreign Minister Maúrtua centered on issues like corruption, economic reactivation, migration management, transnational crime, and the pandemic. It was an agenda reminiscent of the so-called five d's that summarized US policy toward the region and Peru in the Fujimori era (*El Peruano*, 13 November 2021).

At the beginning of 2022, the Biden administration stirred up a hornet's nest throughout the region when it suggested it would only invite democratically elected leaders to the Summit of the Americas in Los Angeles in June 2022. In what appeared to be a turning point in US relations with its neighbors to the south, many of them felt Washington was attempting to turn the clock back to the 1990s. In response, several Latin American heads of state, including Bolivia, Guatemala, Honduras, and Mexico, announced they would not attend if all countries in the hemisphere were not invited, including Cuba, Nicaragua, and Venezuela. "Latin American countries now have China as a partner and feel more empowered to defy the United States and try to occupy a middle ground between the two superpowers.... In other words, to many Latin Americans, this feels like a perfect opportunity to say: No, it's 2022, and we're not going to take this unilateral nonsense from the United States ever again" (Winter 2022, 1–4, quotes 3).

Presidents Castillo and Biden had a positive meeting on the sidelines of the Summit of the Americas, a meeting some observers viewed as a subtle message of support for the Castillo government (Ellis 2022, 15). Four months later, President Castillo and Secretary of State Antony John Blinken met on the sidelines of the OAS General Assembly meeting which took place in Lima in early October 2022 (*La República*, 7 October 2022). Reaching out to the Castillo administration, Secretary Blinken termed Peru "a vital strategic partner" (*El Peruano*, 7 October 2022). Similar to the earlier meeting with Under Secretary Sherman, bilateral talks with President Castillo and Foreign Minister Landa in October 2022 focused on familiar issues, like drug-trafficking, post-pandemic recovery, migration, climate change, and the Venezuelan crisis (United States 2022a). Secretary Blinken also took this opportunity to launch a new policy initiative, *Por la Pesca* (For Fisheries), aimed at assisting the artisanal fishing sector and promoting sustainable fishing in Peru and Ecuador (United States 2022b).

Presidents Castillo and Iván Duque of Colombia also met at the Summit of the Americas and agreed to prioritize the protection of the Amazon Basin from illegal mining and deforestation (*El Peruano*, 7 June 2022). Two days later, nine states bordering on the Pacific Ocean signed a joint declaration aimed at reversing the progressive degradation of the oceans by creating a series of ecologically connected and protected marine zones. After signing the joint declaration, President Castillo rightly emphasized that Peru and the other signatories also needed to do a better job of protecting the streams and rivers that flow into the ocean. (*El Peruano*, 8 June 2022).

Possible New Directions

In April 2021, former Bolivian president Evo Morales announced the birth of RUNASUR (Southern People), an anti-imperialist alternative to UNASUR with a goal of constructing an *América Plurinacional de los Pueblos para los Pueblos* (Plurinational America of the People for the People). When Morales made known plans to hold a RUNASUR forum in Cuzco, Peru on 20–21 December 2021, the Foreign Relations Committee of the Peruvian congress urged President Castillo to declare Morales persona non grata, citing "his negative political activism in Peru" (*Merco Press*, 23 November 2021). Two weeks later, the presidents of the congressional committees for defense, foreign relations, and intelligence issued a joint statement again calling for Morales to be declared persona non grata (*La República*, 12 December 2021).

On 10 December 2021, three of Peru's most experienced and respected former foreign ministers, José García Belaúnde, Ricardo Luna, and Allan Wagner, and eight former vice ministers of foreign affairs issued a joint statement denouncing the planned RUNASUR forum. *Una clara amenaza se aproxima desde el exterior sobre la soberanía, independencia y seguridad nacional*

(A clear threat is approaching from the outside to our national sovereignty, independence, and security). The diplomats also warned that Morales' goal was *desmembrar al Perú otorgando a Bolivia una salida soberana al Pacífico y así conformar un 'nación aymara' como entensión territorial boliviana* (to cut up Peru by granting Bolivia a sovereign exit to the Pacific and thus founding an "Aymara nation" as an extension of Bolivian territory) (*Perú21*, 12 December 2021). In response, the organizers of the Cuzco forum soon announced that it had been suspended but might be held at a later date in Ecuador (*La República*, 12 December 2021).

Having shunned media interviews and avoided public speaking for months, President Castillo agreed to an interview with *CNN Español* in late January 2022. The interview offered an opportunity to clarify the future direction of Peruvian foreign policy; instead, it generated more confusion and controversy. When pressed by his interviewers to say whether or not he believed Cuba, Nicaragua, and Venezuela were dictatorships, Castillo avoided a direct answer, stating he did not want to comment on the domestic affairs of other countries. He responded in a similar fashion when asked whether he recognized Nicolás Maduro or Juan Guaidó as president of Venezuela (*El Comercio*, 26 January 2022). His answer here suggested the Lima Group could no longer count on the Castillo administration for support (Sonneland 2022, 2).

Some observers expressed surprise at Castillo's statement; however, Foreign Minister Maúrtua had signaled an evolution in Peruvian policy toward Venezuela as early as his August 2021 inauguration ceremony. At that time, he said Peru supported the dialogue process in Venezuela and was willing to serve as an alternate venue for meetings among Venezuelan political sectors. Subsequently, the Castillo administration, a few weeks before the CNN interview, welcomed a Maduro-appointed ambassador to Peru as a replacement for the Guaidó-appointed incumbent (*Merco Press*, 29 December 2021). Since the Lima Group was formed in 2017, virtually every country in Latin America except Venezuela had experienced a transition of power, and some including Peru more than one. Yet President Maduro remained in power in Caracas just as he did before the Lima Group was created (Bosworth 2022).

When asked his position on the perennial issue of sovereign Bolivian access to the sea, President Castillo said, *Es una idea. Pero ahora le consultaremos al pueblo* (It is an idea. But now we will consult the [Peruvian] people) (*El Comercio*, 26 January 2022). His response, which implied his government was open to ceding territory to Bolivia, generated a political firestorm in Peru (*Caretas*, 28 January 2022). Earlier, before Castillo had declared himself a candidate for the presidency, he had supported the idea of granting Bolivia access to the sea, and in May 2018, when a candidate for the presidency, Castillo suggested Peru could give Bolivia an outlet to the sea (Ellis 2022, 11).

Hours after Castillo's CNN interview, the Ministry of Foreign Affairs issued a statement that referenced the agreements in place between Bolivia and Peru, notably the 1992 treaty which leased land around Ilo to Bolivia for 99 years and the amplification of that agreement in 2010. While the statement did not mention the president's comments on CNN, it emphasized that any transfer of Peruvian territory to Bolivia would be both unconstitutional and politically impossible (*CNN Español*, 26 January 2022). Addressing congress a few days later, Foreign Minister Maúrtua emphasized, *No es una política de Estado, y por ende tampoco una política del gobierno del president Castillo, promover cesión alguna de territorio peruano* (It is not a State policy [to cede territory to Bolivia] and, therefore, neither is it a policy of President Castillo's government to promote any cession of Peruvian territory) (*El Peruano*, 31 January 2022).

Observers were left to wonder whether Castillo's comments on CNN signaled a future redirection of core elements of Peruvian foreign policy or simply reflected the inexperience of a man who frequently reminded constituents that he was ill prepared to be president. Later in January, opposition members of congress accused President Castillo of treason as a consequence of his CNN interview. Stating that Peruvian territory is both inalienable and unalterable, the legislators argued that the Peruvian constitution prevents standing international agreements from being submitted to a referendum. Thereafter, congress continued to discuss possible charges over Castillo's alleged treason for collaborating with the Bolivian government in its pursuit of sovereign access to the Pacific Ocean (*RPP Noticias*, 20 June 2022).

More of the Same

In the third cabinet shakeup in the first six months of his administration, President Castillo replaced Óscar Maúrtua de Romaña with César Rodrigo Landa Arroyo on 31 January 2022 (*El Peruano*, 31 January 2022). Landa was a highly respected professor of constitutional law at the Catholic University of Peru and the National University of San Marcos but had no recognized experience in foreign affairs. Given his background, Foreign Minister Landa was not expected to initiate radical changes in Peruvian foreign policy. Instead, he wisely focused on familiar issues like ensuring a consistent supply of COVID-19 vaccines, improving relations with neighboring states which he labeled *diplomacia andina*, promoting foreign investment and free-market policies, and improving consular services for Peruvians living abroad. He also pursued wider relations with Brazil and other states in the Amazon River Basin which he referred to as *diplomacia amazónica*, deeper regional relations, and support for more inclusive governance, human rights, and climate change (MREP 2022). The momentum for increased integration with Brazil, an initiative inaugurated during the Toledo administration, slowed in this period under the influence of the Odebrecht scandal, the global pandemic, and the presidency of the far-right, populist Jair Messias Bolsonaro (2019–22).

In an early March 2022 special session of the UN General Assembly, Peru joined 140 other nations in condemning Russia for its invasion of Ukraine. About the same time, Peru under the leadership of UN Ambassador Rodríguez Cuadros co-sponsored a resolution adopted at the fifth session of the UN Environmental Assembly in Nairobi, Kenya establishing an "international negotiating committee (INC) with a mandate to negotiate a legally binding global agreement to address plastic pollution" (UNEP 2022, 1). The resolution addressed the lifecycle of plastic from design to disposal, establishing a path to an international treaty to stop plastic pollution by the end of 2024 (*Reuters*, 2 March 2022).

President Castillo addressed the UN General Assembly in late September 2022, addressing the political crisis in Peru and denouncing coups of all kinds because "they attack the sovereign expression of the people." During his speech, Castillo indicated that Peru would open a representative office in Palestine, characterizing a solution to the conflict between Israel and Palestine as "indispensable." In addition, he reaffirmed the sovereign rights of Argentina over the Islas Malvinas (Falkland Islands), a Peruvian policy as far back as the second Belaúnde Terry administration (1980–85), and he demanded that the parties to the dispute begin consultations to achieve this goal (*El Peruano*, 1 October 2022).

The OECD in June 2022 approved a formal path for Peru and four other states to adhere to the organization (*El Peruano*, 10 June 2022). Historically, the process of accession to the OECD has taken three to seven years from this point. Separately, the British ambassador to Peru in October 2022 announced Peruvians would no longer need a visa to visit the United Kingdom for up to six months, a long-time goal of the Ministry of Foreign Affairs (*El Peruano*, 17 October 2022).

At the end of April 2022, President Castillo joined his Ecuadorian counterpart, Guillermo Lasso, at the 14th Ecuador–Peru presidential and binational cabinet meeting in Loja, Ecuador. At its end, President Lasso stressed that the meeting had succeeded in strengthening both bilateral relations and economic development in border areas. In turn, President Castillo noted that much needed to be done to address common problems like drug trafficking, illegal logging, crime, poverty, and pollution (*Andina*, 30 April 2022). President Castillo then rushed back to Peru by car after bad weather grounded his plane, an incident that highlighted the pettiness of the congress. Castillo risked violating the constitution and giving his opposition in congress an opportunity to impeach him if he failed to return to Peru by midnight Friday, the deadline set by congress when it approved his visit to Ecuador (*Agence France-Presse*, 30 April 2022).

In a further sign of just how strained Castillo's relationship with the opposition-led congress had become, lawmakers in early August 2022 refused permission for the president to travel to Colombia for the inauguration of President-elect Gustavo Francisco Petro Urrego. Peruvian specialists in foreign affairs condemned what they described as an unwise, ill-advised measure. They noted that the president was constitutionally responsible for the foreign policy of Peru; therefore, the decision to deny him permission to travel abroad reflected poorly on Peru, the office of the president, and most especially on the Ministry of Foreign Affairs (*La República*, 7 August 2022). In an unprecedented move, the governments of Argentina, Bolivia, Ecuador, and Mexico in a joint statement spoke out in favor of democracy in Peru, expressing solidarity with legitimately elected authorities and backing a continuation of the Castillo presidency (*Reuters*, 12 August 2022). A public opinion poll released the same day that congress blocked Castillo's travel plans to Colombia indicated the chief executive's approval rating was up slightly to 24 percent while that of congress was at a new low of 10 percent (*La República*, 7 August 2022).

In yet another cabinet shakeup, President Castillo on 5 August 2022 replaced Foreign Minister César Rodrigo Landa Arroyo with Miguel Ángel Rodríguez Mackay, the fourth person named to the post since the beginning of the Castillo administration less than 13 months earlier (*Perú21*, 6 August 2022). President of the Peruvian Institute of International Law and International Relations, Rodríguez Mackay was an internationalist but not a career diplomat. Within days of his appointment, he announced two controversial decisions. First, in a nod to the territorial integrity of Morocco, he reversed a decision taken one year earlier by the Ministry of Foreign Affairs and withdrew Peruvian recognition of the Sahrawi Arab Democratic Republic (SADR). At the same time, Rodríguez Mackay voiced support for an autonomy plan announced earlier by the Moroccan government. Second, he shelved the environmental agreement known as the Escazú Accord. The Peruvian left, notably Vladimir Cerrón Rojas's Perú Libre and Verónika Mendoza's New Perú, strongly criticized both decisions and called for Rodríguez Mackay's resignation. Upwards of 100 organizations, institutions, and other parties focused on climate and environmental issues also condemned the decision not to proceed with ratification of the Escazú Accord, arguing Rodríguez Mackay should resign if he did not reverse it (*La República*,

19 August 2022). Shortly thereafter, Foreign Minister Rodríguez Mackay suggested that Peru should sign the controversial Convención de las Naciones Unidas sobre el Derecho del Mar (CONVEMAR) (*El Comercio*, 9 September 2022). The Peruvian government had long refused to sign this 1982 document on the grounds its terms compromised its claim since 1952 to a 200 nautical mile territorial sea, and among other things, could increase competition for the artisanal fishing sector (St John 1999b, 180–81).

Foreign Minister Rodríguez Mackay resigned after 36 days in office, a tenure twice as long as that of Héctor Béjar, a questionable benchmark (*El Peruano*, 8 September 2022). To replace him, President Castillo reappointed César Rodrigo Landa Arroyo a little over a month after he had sacked him (*La República*, 14 September 2022). One of Landa's first acts was to reappoint Ambassador José Manuel Rodríguez Cuadros as Peru's UN representative and Ambassador Harold Forsyth as Peru's OAS representative. Both diplomats had resigned from their posts in August to protest the appointment of Rodríguez Mackay as foreign minister (*La República*, 15 September 2022). The Castillo administration also quickly reaffirmed its support for SADR, the Escazú Accord, and a 200 nautical mile territorial sea (*El Comercio*, 13 September 2022).

From Castillo to Boluarte

In a country in which political parties were extremely weak and fragmented, President Castillo repeatedly restructured the government to curry favor among specific groups in a constant effort to avoid being removed from office. In his first 13 months in office, he faced down two attempts to impeach him, reshuffled his government four times, and appointed more than 80 cabinet ministers, an average of one new minister named every six days of the Castillo presidency (*La República*, 25 August 2022).

With the congress set to debate a third vacancy motion, President Castillo announced on 7 December 2022 that he was dissolving congress, declaring a state of emergency, and ruling by decree (*El Comercio*, 7 December 2022). Castillo's attempt to dissolve the congress echoed a similar move three decades earlier by President Alberto Fujimori who successfully staged an *autogolpe* (self coup) in 1992 and shut down the congress with the support of the military. In Castillo's case, he lacked both the constitutional authority and the political support necessary to succeed. His surprise declaration was widely denounced as an attempted coup, members of his cabinet resigned and the country's armed forces and national police rejected the move. Within a couple of hours, President Castillo was arrested for the "alleged crime of rebellion" and incarcerated (*La República*, 8 December 2022).

Vice President Dina Ercilia Boluarte Zegarra, a 60-year-old lawyer from Apurímac in the south-central Andes, was sworn in as the constitutional successor to Castillo, the first woman to hold the office. Earlier, she had been expelled from the Perú Libre party and had distanced herself from left-wing groups in congress. With no political party, no natural allies, and little political support, President Boluarte was tasked with governing a country that had five presidents in five years. President Boluarte appointed a largely technical cabinet, including Ambassador Ana Cecilia Gervasi Díaz as Minister of Foreign Affairs, in an effort to calm political passions and restore stability throughout Peru (*La República*, 11 December 2022). Foreign Minister Gervasi was a career diplomat with extensive experience, including as a vice minister of foreign affairs (*El Peruano*, 9 December 2022). Over the next few weeks, her activities focused on persuading neighboring states and the international community that the Boluarte government was in control of a chaotic situation and would soon restore a degree of normalcy (*El Peruano*, 1 February 2023). Her job was not made easier by the resignation "due to the rupture of democratic and constitutional order" of former foreign minister Rodríguez Cuadros as Peru's UN representative and Ambassador Forsyth as Peru's OAS representative (*Andina*, 9 January 2023). In addition, the Boluarte government dismissed several ambassadors appointed by the Castillo administration, including former foreign minister Maúrtua de Romaña as Peruvian ambassador to Spain and Andorra (*La República*, 28 January 2023).

Immediately following Boluarte's elevation to the presidency, widespread and violent demonstrations, led mainly by indigenous, rural, and poorer Peruvians, began in the Andean highlands, later reaching Lima (*Associated Press*, 20 January 2023). By the end of January 2023, at least 58 people were dead, almost all of them civilians, and hundreds more were injured (*Perú21*, 30 January 2023). As a measure of the seriousness of the situation, President Merino resigned in November 2020 after only two protestors died. The demonstrators demanded Boluarte's resignation, national elections, and a constituent assembly. President Boluarte and other officials responded with the almost laughable argument that the most violent demonstrations were organized by criminal groups, terrorists, RUNASUR, illegal miners, smugglers, drug traffickers, and Sendero Luminoso (*La República*, 6 January 2023). Foreign Minister Gervasi later admitted in a *New York Times* interview that the government had no proof of these allegations, adding she was "sure that we will have that evidence very soon" (*New York Times*, 3 February 2023).

In its effort to position itself as the symbol of order, the Boluarte administration and the congress failed to acknowledge the deeper socioeconomic and political motivations of the demonstrators, grievances that reflected a system that had failed to deliver for the two decades since democracy was restored in 2001 (*La República*, 4 February 2023). Outwardly, Peruvians mostly demonstrated for political change, including a new president, congress, and constitution (*La República*, 30 December 2022). Inwardly, many also demonstrated for a more equitable socioeconomic and political system that reflected the progressive, redistributive, and fiscal policies President Castillo promised but failed to deliver (*New York Times*, 17 January 2023).

In a poll conducted by the Instituto de Estudios Peruanos (IEP), one of the most respected NGOs in Peru, 89 percent of respondents disapproved of congress, 76 percent disapproved of President Boluarte, 73 percent favored national elections in 2023, and 69 percent favored a constituent assembly (*La República*, 29 January 2023). Seven weeks into a self-styled government of dialogue and transition, the Centro Estratégico Latinoamericano Geopolítica (CELAG) noted that the Boluarte administration had the second highest death toll of any Latin American government in this century, second only to that of the right-wing Colombian government of Iván Duque Márquez (*La República*, 29 January 2023). In the midst of the chaos, President Boluarte designated 2023 as the *Año de la unidad, la paz y el desarrollo* (Year of unity, peace, and development) (*La República*, 20 January 2023). Whether or not she could deliver on that promise remained to be seen.

Concluding Observations

During the presidential campaign, candidate Castillo promised radical change in domestic and foreign policies; however, once in office, he proved unable to implement them. A political novice, he ran afoul of many of the same institutional, socioeconomic, and political constraints that had frustrated his immediate predecessors. Poor judgment, corruption, and personal foibles compounded issues of governance. For a time, Castillo proved himself a political survivor but only because he jettisoned the radical policies he promised on the campaign trail. This was especially true in the realm of foreign policy where the priorities of the foreign ministry remained solidly grounded in the recognized, long term interests of Peru. The eventual fate of the Boluarte administration remained unclear as well as the domestic and foreign policies it might follow if it was able to cling to power. In any case, the evidence available suggests Peruvian foreign policy will continue to be characterized by a mix of continuity and change with continuity generally trumping change.

Chapter 8

CONCLUSIONS

In common with most of its neighbors, the foreign policy of Peru after independence in 1821 focused on core interests that can be summarized as political sovereignty, territorial integrity, continental solidarity, and economic independence. Over the next 200 years, Peruvian foreign policy expanded in scope and direction; nevertheless, these four tenets continued to encapsulate the nation's external policy. Consequently, the permanent interests of Peru remain a logical place to begin an assessment of Peruvian foreign policy in the modern era.

Political Sovereignty

In the early years of independence, Peru struggled to decide whether it would divide, federate with Bolivia, or stand alone. Like most newly independent states, Peru achieved statehood long before it achieved nationhood, and it sometimes struggled to retain the former as it strived to develop the latter. From the outset, the Peruvian Diplomat Service played a decisive role in the legal defense of the national inheritance often in vast, encyclopedic defenses of Peruvian territorial claims. Over time, Peru faced nine wars (two with Chile, two with Colombia, two with Ecuador, and three with Bolivia). After each one, Peruvian diplomats negotiated a peace mostly on terms favorable to Peru. Having achieved political sovereignty in the nineteenth century, there was little serious challenge to it, apart from a few territorial issues, in the twentieth century.

The issue of political sovereignty surfaced again during the Castillo administration. In late 2021, former Bolivian president Evo Morales announced his intention to hold a meeting in Cuzco of RUNASUR, an organization that entertained vague plans of constructing a plurinational nation from Bolivia, Ecuador, and Peru. In response to efforts to organize the Cuzco gathering, the Foreign Relations Committee of the Peruvian congress condemned what it termed the political activism of Morales and called for President Castillo to declare Morales persona non grata. A few days later, three former foreign ministers and eight former vice foreign ministers issued a joint statement denouncing the proposed RUNASUR forum as a clear threat to the national sovereignty, independence, and security of Peru. The Cuzco forum was later postponed; nevertheless, the declared objectives of RUNASUR remained a latent threat to the political sovereignty of Peru. The RUNASUR issue surfaced again during the demonstrations that swept Peru in 2022–23. Initially, President Boluarte and other officials claimed without evidence that RUNASUR supporters had infiltrated the demonstrations to sow discord in Peru.

Territorial Integrity

At independence, Peru faced threats to its territorial integrity from all sides. At one time or another, Bolivia, Brazil, Chile, Colombia, and Ecuador coveted lands and waters that the newly-formed Republic of Peru considered its own. To the credit of Peruvian diplomacy, the nation was remarkably successful over the next two centuries in protecting its territorial integrity. Often criticized, the final settlements to its many territorial and maritime disputes maintained the territorial essence of Peru. Settlements with Brazil and Colombia involved some loss of territory, but it was largely land over which Peru lacked solid legal or other claims. Minimal territory was ceded to Bolivia, and in the Ecuadorian case, Peru eventually retained most of the land in dispute. In reality, the bulk of the territory lost by Peru after 1821 was the result of interstate conflict, notably the War of the Pacific, as opposed to any real or imaginary shortcomings of Peruvian diplomacy. For perspective, the success of Peru in protecting its territorial integrity can be compared to Bolivia which today is less than half the area it claimed at independence (St John 2020).

The Fujimori administration negotiated a settlement to the seemingly intractable territorial dispute with Ecuador and also concluded a package of agreements with Chile that resolved outstanding issues from the 1929 Tacna and Arica Treaty and Additional Protocol. The Toledo administration initiated a legal process before the International Court of Justice at The Hague which concluded during the Humala administration with an award that ended its maritime dispute with Chile on terms generally favorable to Peru. In the interim, the García administration resolved outstanding maritime issues with Ecuador. With long-standing territorial and maritime issues ending, Peruvian diplomacy shifted its focus to cooperative efforts in the borderlands, skillfully employing the binational cabinet meeting format to focus on issues like border security, economic development, and transnational crime, while also working to improve support and services for

Peruvians abroad. In addition, social diplomacy for the first time became a stated goal of Peruvian foreign policy, highlighting the growing realization that domestic policy in an expanding era of globalization was increasingly a function of foreign policy and vice-versa. In the Toledo administration, Foreign Minister Manuel Rodríguez Cuadros was an ardent proponent of the use of social diplomacy to combat poverty through increased participation in multilateral bodies concerned with socioeconomic development.

With the conclusion of the Chile-Peru maritime dispute, the process of delimiting the land and sea boundaries of Peru that began with independence was thought to have been concluded. Therefore, it surprised most observers when the dialogue surrounding the proposed RUNASUR forum in Cuzco included the prospect of giving Bolivia sovereign access to the Pacific Ocean through Peru. When a CNN reporter in January 2022 asked President Castillo about his position on a Bolivian seaport, his response suggested his government might be open to ceding territory to Bolivia. Castillo's response, which was consistent with his earlier comments on the issue, generated a political firestorm in Peru. Hours after Castillo's CNN interview, the Ministry of Foreign Affairs issued a statement emphasizing that any transfer of Peruvian territory to Bolivia would be both unconstitutional and politically impossible. In addressing the congress a few days later, Foreign Minister Maúrtua stressed that the cession of territory to Bolivia was not a policy of the state or government. Although Maúrtua's statement appeared to close the matter, members of the opposition in congress, in a move highlighting the recurrent impact of domestic politics on Peruvian foreign policy, continued to explore the possibility of charging President Castillo with treason over his seeming support for a Bolivian seaport.

Continental Solidarity

Over the last three decades, Peru has maintained its long-standing commitment to continental solidarity as evidenced by its active participation in subregional, regional, and international organizations. Peruvian participation in the United Nations and the Organization of American States goes back to their founding in 1945 and 1948, respectively, and it joined the Latin American Free Trade Association when it was created in 1960. In all of these organizations, Peru was a voice for reform, especially in the United Nations, where it has long advocated reforms to the UN collective security system, including an increase in the number of Security Council members and the elimination of the veto power of permanent members.

Peru also was active in a growing number of new international organizations and institutions like the European Union, Latin America and the Caribbean Summit, Organization of Ibero–American States, and the South American–Arab Countries Summit. Membership in these bodies was often more symbolic than tangible in benefit. At the same time, they offered opportunities for senior Peruvian officials to meet their counterparts from other countries, contributing indirectly or directly to broader commercial and diplomatic ties with states outside Latin America and the Caribbean.

Successive Peruvian governments were especially active in Asia. During the Fujimori administration, Peru joined the Pacific Basin Economic Council in 1990, the Pacific Economic Cooperation Council in 1991, and the Asia-Pacific Economic Cooperation forum in 1998. During the García administration, Peru hosted both the 16th Summit of the APEC Forum and the 5th Summit of Heads of State and Government of Latin America, the Caribbean, and the European Union. It also joined the Pacific Alliance in 2011. Important bilateral agreements concluded in this period included but were not limited to Ecuador (1998), Brazil (2003), China (2008), and the European Union (2009).

Some of the regional or subregional bodies in which Peru played a prominent role over the last 30 years included the Andean Community of Nations, South American Community of Nations, Union of South American Nations, Community of Latin America and Caribbean States, and Forum for the Progress and Integration of South America. Economic concerns were the core agenda of most of these organizations; however, Peru often succeeded in using them to advance political agendas, notably support for democracy and human rights, regional arms control, and reform at the United Nations. Examples of the important leadership role played by Peru in these bodies included sponsorship for the Inter-American Democratic Charter (2001), Cuzco Consensus (2003), Andean Zone of Peace (2004), Declaration of Nuevo León (2004), Lima Group (2017), Lima Commitment (2017), and Global Treaty Ending Plastic Pollution (2022).

Economic Independence

Economic independence remained a core goal of Peruvian foreign policy in the modern era. The Fujimori administration implemented generally orthodox economic policies, emphasizing free trade and market reforms, and since that time, the Peruvian economy has continued to rely on export-led growth. The Peruvian economy at independence was geared to agricultural and mineral export, and the Peruvian economy in the twenty-first century is still geared to agricultural and mineral export. *Plus ça change, plus c'est la même chose* (The more things change, the more they remain the same). With China, the European Union, and the United States as key trade partners, foreign policy and trade policy remain inextricably intertwined.

With the US footprint in Latin America in general and Peru, in particular, lighter, less distinct, and less forceful than it had been for many decades, Peru naturally looked to Asia and Europe as well as Brazil to diversify exports, develop human capital, and modernize infrastructure. In this sense, it was not political policies or crises but the economic opportunity presented by China and the European Union that altered Peru's stance toward the United States over the last two decades. Concomitant with its growing presence in the region, China is positioned to play an increasingly important economic and political role in Peru and neighboring states. Moreover, the reorientation both in trade and investment policies and trade partners taking place can be expected to continue as exemplified by the Trade Agreement between Colombia, Ecuador, and Peru and the European Union and Its Member States (2012), Peruvian membership in the Trans-Pacific Partnership (2016) and the ever deepening commercial relationship between China and Peru.

Domestic and Foreign Policy

In Peru, internal politics and external policies have been inseparable since independence with international economics and national economic development frequently representing the clearest nexus between domestic and foreign policy. From the beginning, Peruvian decision-makers rightly viewed domestic policy as the main concern of their constituents; consequently, foreign policy was often influenced if not shaped by domestic concerns and considerations. Conversely, opportunistic politicians with limited domestic support sometimes stressed foreign policy issues to divert attention from domestic political crises. In the same vein, issues of internal economic growth and development have long had more salience in Peru than the latest Super Power conflict. The close link between domestic and foreign policy was obvious in all of the presidential administrations after 1990 but especially in the Fujimori and Castillo governments. To exemplify the importance of internal politics to foreign policy, one need only examine the common fate of Peruvian chief executives after 1985.

With the exception of interim President Valentín Paniagua (2000–2001), every Peruvian president between 1985 and 2023 has been imprisoned, impeached, or pursued in criminal investigations. In 2009, Alberto Fujimori was convicted of human rights violations and sentenced to 25 years in jail. Pardoned in 2017, he returned to jail in 2019 after his pardon was canceled. In 2022, the Constitutional Court voted to restore Fujimori's pardon; however, the Inter-American Court of Human Rights intervened, and Fujimori again returned to jail. Ollanta Humala and his wife, Nadine Heredia, upon leaving office faced charges of both accepting illegal campaign donations and money laundering. In February 2022, Humala became the first former Peruvian president to go on trial in the corruption case involving the Brazilian conglomerate Odebrecht and the bribes it paid to politicians in Peru and elsewhere. In September 2021, a San Francisco judge cleared the way for Alejandro Toledo, charged with taking US$34 million in bribes from Odebrecht and another US$4 million from the Brazilian company Camargo Correa to be extradited to Peru.

In April 2019, Pedro-Pablo Kuczynski was placed in preventive detention based on charges his financial services firm took money from Odebrecht while he was serving as prime minister in the Toledo government. When authorities in 2019 attempted to arrest Alan García in connection with the Odebrecht scandal, he shot himself in the head later dying in a hospital. In late 2021, Martín Vizcarra was banned from public office for 10 years following charges of taking bribes while serving as governor of Moquegua and of being vaccinated in a COVID-19 trial in which he was not an official participant. After serving as president for five days, Manuel Merino was charged with abuse of authority and the death of two protesters during a violent crackdown of demonstrations against the ouster of Vizcarra. In October 2018, Keiko Fujimori, accused of faking campaign fundraising events to disguise illicit Odebrecht donations, joined the list of politicians charged with criminal activities, including money laundering. Subsequently, her false claims of electoral fraud in the 2021 presidential election led to new criminal investigations against her. Finally, the administration of Pedro Castillo was mired in corruption and scandal from the outset, including multiple allegations of criminal activities by the president himself. In November 2022, Barómetro de las Américas, a scientifically rigorous comparative study of the Americas, ranked Peru number one in terms of the highest perceived level of political corruption in Latin America. President Castillo was later detained on charges of attempting to illegally dissolve congress, and his successor, Dina Boluarte, soon faced charges for genocide, qualified homicide, and serious injury stemming from widespread demonstrations that left dozens of civilians dead and hundreds injured.

Continuity and Change

The foreign policy of most states is a balance between continuity and change with the equilibrium shifting as challenges, opportunities, and crises come and go. Peruvian foreign policy after 1990 is an excellent example of this constant balancing act between continuity and change. After almost three decades of experimentation, the Fujimori administration returned to more traditional interests and concerns in a foreign policy that favored continuity but did not forego change. Once his orthodox economic policies began to bear fruit, President Fujimori introduced creative new initiatives which shifted the direction, content, and tone of Peruvian foreign policy. Selected elements of this transition included increased support for free trade and market reforms; renewed commitment to subregional, regional, and international cooperation; recognition of the changing role of the United States in world politics; and a resultant commitment to wider, deeper relations with Asia and Europe. Successive presidential administrations from Toledo to Castillo refined and cultivated these initiatives in a foreign policy characterized more by continuity than change, but one in which the capability to effect change within continuity was a hallmark of Peruvian diplomacy. As former foreign minister Ricardo Luna aptly observed, "It is the effort to maintain the capacity to innovate within geopolitical and historical fetters that has made Peruvian diplomacy in the last fifty years largely successful" (Luna Mendoza, interview with author, 24 July 2022).

Peruvian Diplomatic Service

The remarkable breadth and depth of contemporary Peruvian foreign policy is a testimony to the professionalism of the Peruvian Diplomatic Service. Over the last three decades, Peruvian diplomats successfully addressed a number of crises in large part due to astute diplomacy. They picked their battles well, and for the most part, they contested issues on which they had substantial domestic and regional backing. Today, the Peruvian Diplomatic Service is staffed with a first-rate corps of experienced, full-time professionals. Two-thirds of the men and women who served as minister of foreign affairs in the twenty-first century were professional diplomats. Moreover, modifications to the statutes governing the diplomatic service enacted during the Paniagua, Toledo, and García administrations, coupled with a strong faculty and demanding curriculum at the Peruvian Diplomatic Academy, ensure a pipeline of highly trained and capable future diplomats. Earning university status in 2005, the Diplomatic Academy is now the sole entry point into the Peruvian Diplomatic Service. Highly respected by peers in the region and throughout the world, the Peruvian Diplomatic Service remains well-placed both to promote the international interests of Peru and to support the needs of Peruvians abroad.

Conclusion

Political sovereignty, territorial integrity, continental solidarity, and economic independence have been goals of Peruvian foreign policy since the declaration of independence in 1821, and two centuries later, they remain useful gauges of Peruvian foreign policy in the modern era. Peruvian governments from Fujimori to Boluarte have skillfully employed a combination of continuity and change to implement a foreign policy grounded in pragmatism and notable for rational, consistent, and generally achievable initiatives that mostly complement and support each other. At the same time, the restoration of the integrity and professionalism of the Peruvian Diplomatic Service following the scandal of the 1990s ensured that successive governments after 2000 had the necessary diplomatic skills and tools available to them to pursue successfully new initiatives in a rapidly changing global milieu.

WORKS CITED

Books, Articles, Documents

Adins, Sebastién. 2015. "La posición peruana frente a la UNASUR y la CELAC." In *La política exterior peruana en el siglo XXI: Agenda y propuestas*, coordinator Fabián Novak and Jaime García, 245–62. Lima: Fondo Editorial de la Pontificia Universidad Católica del Perú and Konrad Adenauer Stiftung.

Adins, Sebastién and Mildred Rooney. 2019. *The Relations between Peru and the Russian Federation: Revision and Interpretation from an International Relations Perspective.* Lima: Konrad Adenauer Stiftung and Instituto de Estudios Internacionales, Pontificia Universidad Católica del Perú.

Aguirre, Carlos and Paulo Drinot, eds. 2017. *The Peculiar Revolution: Rethinking the Peruvian Experiment under Military Rule.* Austin: University of Texas Press.

Alden, Christopher and Alvaro Méndez. 2019. "Perú, China y la nueva multipolaridad – navegar en la política internacional en tiempos inciertos." In *La conexión China en la Política Exterior del Perú en el siglo XXI*, ed. Alvaro Méndez, Javier Alcade and Christopher Alden, 278–307. Lima: Fondo Editorial de la Pontificia Universidad Católica del Perú.

Alurralde Tejada, Juan Carlos, Jorge Molina, Elena Villarroel and Paula Pacheco. 2011. "Science helps to solve international water conflicts case: The Mauri River." Paper presented at XIV World Water Congress, Pernambuco, Brazil (25–29 September). https://www.iwra.org/member/congress/resource/PAP00-5666.pdf.

Ancient Civilizations Forum. 2017. "Athens Ministerial Conference on the Formation of the Ancient Civilization Forum." Athens, Greece (23–24 April). https://ancientcivilizationsforum.org/.

Aramayo, Carlos and Carlos Pereira. 2011. "Brazil's Influence in Peru's 2011 Election." Brookings Institution (14 June). https://www.brookings.edu/opinions/brazils-influence-in-perus-2011-presidential-election/.

Autoridad Nacional del Agua. Dirección de Conservación y Planeamiento de Recursos Hídricos. 2015. *Model hidrológico de la Cuenca Maure-Mauri: Anexos.* Lima: Ministerio de Desarrollo Agrario y Riego. https://repositorio.ana.gob.pe/handle/20.500.12543/1931.

Avery, William P. 1983. "The Politics of Crisis and Cooperation in the Andean Group." *Journal of Developing Areas* 17, 2 (January): 156–65.

Ayuso, Anna, Santiago Villar, Camila Pastor and Miguel Fuentes. 2018. "Actors and Opportunities: Interregional Processes in the Arab Region and Latin America and the Caribbean." In *Interregionalism across the Atlantic Space*, ed. Frank Mattheis and Andréas Litsegard, 51–74. New York: Springer.

Bákula Patiño, Juan Miguel. 2002. *Perú: entre la realidad y la utopía, 180 años de política exterior.* 2 vols. Lima: Fondo de Cultura Económica and Fundación Academia Diplomática del Perú.

Béjar Rivera, Héctor. 1969. *Peru 1965: Notes on a Guerrilla Experience.* New York: Monthly Review Press.

Berenson, Mark L. 2005. "Peru vs. Lori Berenson: The Case Continues." *NACLA Report on the Americas* 38, 5 (25 September): 4–5. https://nacla.org/article/peru-vs-lori-berenson-case-continues.

Bilotta, Nicola. 2018. *The Legacy of Post-Neoliberal Integration in South America: The Cases of ALBA and UNASUR.* Istituto Affari Internazionali. Paper No. 18/20 (December). https://www.iai.it/en/pubblicazioni/legacy-post-neoliberal-integration-south-america-cases-alba-and-unasur.

Ble, Martha Guerrero, Izza Leghtas and Jimmy Graham. 2020. *From Displacement to Development: How Peru Can Transform Venezuela Displacement into Shared Growth.* Case Study. Center for Global Displacement and Refugees International (December). https://www.cgdev.org/publication/displacement-development-how-peru-can-transform-venezuelan-displacement-shared-growth.

Bonilla, Heraclio. 1974. *Guano y Burguesía en el Perú.* Lima: Instituto de Estudios Peruanos.

———. 1980. *Un siglo a la deriva: Ensayos sobre el Perú, Bolivia y la guerra.* Lima: Instituto de Estudios Peruanos.

Bosworth, James. 2022. "Latin America Needs to Learn From the Lima Group's Failure on Venezuela." *World Politics Review* (29 August). https://www.worldpoliticsreview.com/maduro-venezuela-lima-group-latin-america-dictatorships/.

Bragatti, Milton Carlos. 2019. "Ten Years of the South American Defense Council: Regional International Security Architecture." *Geopolítica* 10, 1 (April): 69–86.

Brousset Barrios, Jorge. 2012. "Política exterior y asuntos marítimos." In *Veinte años de política exterior peruana (1991–2011)*, coordinator Fabián Novak, 321–44. Lima: Fondo Editorial de la Pontificia Universidad Católica del Perú.

Burt, Jo-Marie. 2008. "Fujimori on Trial." *NACLA Report on the Americas* 41, 3 (May/June): 10–14. https://nacla.org/article/fujimori-trial.

———. 2020. "Can Francisco Sagasti Hold Peru Together?" *Americas Quarterly* (19 November). https://www.americasquarterly.org/article/can-francisco-sagasti-hold-peru-together/.

Cameron, Maxwell. 2019. "From Oligarchic Domination to Neoliberal Governance: The Shining Path and the Transformation of Peru's Constitutional Order." In *Politics after Violence: Legacies of the Shining Path Conflict in Peru*, ed. Hillel David Soifer and Alberto Vergara, 79–108. Austin: University of Texas Press.

Camilleri, Michael J. 2020. "Biden's Latin American Opportunity." *Foreign Affairs* (28 December). https://www.foreignaffairs.com/articles/central-america-caribbean/2020-12-28/bidens-latin-american-opportunity.

Cardenal, Juan Pablo. 2017. "Reframing Relations in Peru." In *Sharp Power: Rising Authoritarian Influence*, 67–93. Washington, DC: National Endowment for Democracy. https://www.ned.org/wp-content/uploads/2017/12/Sharp-Power-Rising-Authoritarian-Influence-Full-Report.pdf.

Clayton, Lawrence A. 1999. *Peru and the United States: The Condor and the Eagle.* Athens and London: University of Georgia Press.

Cobas, Efraín. 1982. *Fuerza armada, misiones militares y dependencia en el Perú.* Lima: Editorial Horizonte.

Crabtree, John. 1992. *Peru under García: An Opportunity Lost.* Pittsburgh, PA: University of Pittsburgh Press.

———. 2006. "Political Parties and Intermediation in Peru." In *Making Institutions Work in Peru*, ed. John Crabtree, 24–44. London: Institute for the Study of the Americas, University of London.

Crabtree, John and Francisco Durand. 2017. *Peru: Elite Power and Political Capture.* London: Zed Books.

Denegri Luna, Félix. 1996. *Peru and Ecuador: Notes for the History of a Frontier.* Lima: Instituto Riva-Agüero and Pontificia Universidad Católica del Perú.

De Trazegnies Granda, Fernando. 2012. "Las relaciones entre Perú y Ecuador: caminando juntos." In *Veinte años de política exterior peruana (1991–2011)*, coordinator Fabián Novak, 43–51. Lima: Fondo Editorial de la Pontificia Universidad Católica del Perú.

De Zela, Hugo. 2012. "Las relaciones entre Perú y Brasil: La profundización de la alianza estratégica." In *Veinte años de política exterior peruana (1991–2011)*, coordinator Fabián Novak, 15–41. Lima: Fondo Editorial de la Pontificia Universidad Católica del Perú.

Dunkelberg, Alonso Gurmendi. 2020. "What Just Happened in Peru? Understanding Vizcarra's Sudden Impeachment." *Americas Quarterly* (10 November). https://www.americasquarterly.org/article/what-just-happened-in-peru-understanding-vizcarras-sudden-impeachment/.

Ellis, Evan. 2022. "The Evolution of Peru's Multidimensional Challenges, Part I: The Political Crisis." *Global Americas* (13 July). https://theglobalamericans.org/2022/07/the-evolution-of-perus-multidimensional-challenges-part-i-the-political-crisis/.

Erikson, Daniel P. 2018. "Make the Summit of the Americas Great Again." *Foreign Policy* (20 April). https://foreignpolicy.com/2018/04/20/make-the-summit-of-the-americas-great-again/.

Eshleman, Clayton, ed. 2007. *The Complete Poetry of César Vallejo.* Berkeley, CA: University of California Press.

Faundez, Julio. 2019. *The International Court of Justice and Maritime Disputes: The Case of Chile and Peru.* London and New York: Routledge.

Ferrero Costa, Eduardo. 1987. "Peruvian Foreign Policy: Current Trends, Constraints and Opportunities." *Journal of Interamerican Studies and World Affairs* 29, 2 (Summer): 55–78.

———. 2018. *Perú–Ecuador: el proceso para lograr la Paz.* Lima: Fondo Editorial de la Pontificia Universidad Católica del Perú.

Flannery, Nathaniel Parish. 2013. "How China's Relations with Peru Explain Its Approach to Diplomacy." *The Atlantic* (12 September). https://www.theatlantic.com/china/archive/2013/09/how-chinas-relations-with-peru-explain-its-approach-to-diplomacy/279618/.

Fuentes Cervantes, Miguel. 2018. "Notes on Foreign Policy Responses to China: The Cases of Chile, Ecuador and Peru." *Política Internacional* 126 (January-December): 34–48.

García, Jaime. 2012. "Relaciones económicos y comerciales entre el Perú y los países árabes." In *Veinte años de política exterior peruana (1991–2011)*, coordinator Fabián Novak, 243–69. Lima: Fondo Editorial de la Pontificia Universidad Católica del Perú.

García Belaúnde, José Antonio. 2014. "Delímites y precisions: El largo camino a La Haya." *El Comercio* (29 January). http://3.elcomercio.e3.pe/doc/0/0/8/1/7/817213.pdf.

————. 2021. *Dos siglos de desafíos en la política exterior peruana*. Lima: Ministerio de Cultura - Proyecto Especial Bicentenario de Independencia del Perú.

García-Corrochano, Luis. 2012. "La política exterior del Perú respecto de Bolivia y Chile (1992–2012)." In *Veinte años de política exterior peruana (1991–2011)*, coordinator Fabián Novak, 75–94. Lima: Fondo Editorial de la Pontificia Universidad Católica del Perú.

García-Sayán Larrabure, Diego. 2002. *Una nueva política exterior peruana: Democrática, moderna, independiente y al servicio de la gente*. Lima: Comisión Andina de Juristas and Academia Diplomática del Perú.

Garibaldi de Mendoza, Rosa. 2003. *La política exterior del Perú en la era de Ramón Castilla: Defensa hemisférica y defensa de la jurisdicción nacional*. Lima: Fundación Academia Diplomática del Perú.

González Vigil, Fernando. 2012. "Relaciones de comercio e inversión del Perú con el Asia-Pacífico." In *Veinte años de política exterior peruana (1991–2011)*, coordinator Fabián Novak, 209–41. Lima: Fondo Editorial de la Pontificia Universidad Católica del Perú.

Goodman, Jonathan. 2018. "Where does Perú go from here: The Fujimori Blessing to Martín Vizcarra's Presidency." Council on Hemispheric Affairs (10 July). https://www.coha.org/where-does-peru-go-from-here-the-fujimori-blessing-to-martin-vizcarras-presidency/.

Hooker, Silvia. 2015. "Las relaciones del Perú con Asia: Posibilidades en APEC y el TPP." In *La política exterior peruana en el siglo XXI: Agenda y propuestas*, coordinator Fabián Novak and Jaime García, 191–203. Lima: Fondo Editorial de la Pontificia Universidad Católica del Perú and Konrad Adenauer Stiftung.

Horler, Stephan and Ruby Cazarez. 2016. "Peru 2016 Presidential Elections: César Acuña and Julio Guzmán Disqualified." Council on Hemispheric Affairs (15 March). https://www.coha.org/peru-2016-presidential-elections-cesar-acuna-and-julio-guzman-disqualified/.

Humala Tasso, Ollanta. 2009. *De locumba a candidato a la presidencia en Perú*. Lima: Ocean Sur.

Iguíñez, Javier. 1998. "The Economic Strategy of the Fujimori Government." In *Fujimori's Peru: The Political Economy*, ed. John Crabtree and Jim Thomas, 24–40. London: Institute of Latin American Studies, University of London.

International Court of Justice (ICJ). 2014. *Maritime Dispute (Peru v. Chile): Judgment*, General List No. 137. The Hague (27 January). https://www.icj-cij.org/public/files/case-related/137/137-20140127-JUD-01-00-EN.pdf.

International Monetary Fund (IMF). 2022. "Staff Report for the 2022 Article IV Consultation." Washington, DC (13 April). https://www.imf.org/en/Publications/CR/Issues/2022/05/11/Peru-2022-Article-IV-Consultation-Press-Release-Staff-Report-and-Statement-by-the-Executive-517828.

Jaworski C., Hélan. 1984. "Peru: The Military Government's Foreign Policy in Its Two Phases (1968–1980)." In *Latin American Nations in World Politics*, ed. Heraldo Muñoz and Joseph S. Tulchin, 200–15. Boulder and London: Westview.

Kahhat, Farid. 2015. "Relaciones recientes de América Latina, el Caribe y el Perú con el Medio Oriente." In *La política exterior peruana en el siglo XXI: Agenda y propuestas*, coordinator Fabián Novak and Jaime García, 125–32. Lima: Fondo Editorial de la Pontificia Universidad Católica del Perú and Konrad Adenauer Stiftung.

Kenney, Charles D. 2004. *Fujimori's Coup and the Breakdown of Democracy in Latin America*. Notre Dame, IN: University of Notre Dame Press.

Kuczynski, Pedro-Pablo. 1977. *Peruvian Democracy under Economic Stress: An Account of the Belaúnde Administration, 1963–1968*. Princeton NJ: Princeton University Press.

———. 2016. "Mensaje a la Nación del Señor Presidente Constitucional de la República Señor Pedro Pablo Kuczynski Godard." Lima (28 July). https://www.congreso.gob.pe/Docs/participacion/museo/congreso/files/mensajes/2001-2020/files/mensaje-2017-ppk.pdf.

Larraín, Felipe and Pepe Zhang. 2023. "China's Evolving Presence in Latin America." *Americas Quarterly* (3 January). https://www.americasquarterly.org/article/china-is-here-to-stay-in-latin-america/#.

León Collazos, G. 2018. "Los gabinetes binacionales como herramienta política en la Cooperación Sur-Sur: El caso del Perú y Colombia." *Zero* 35 (28 February). https://zero.uexternado.edu.co/los-gabinetes-binacionales-como-herramienta-politica-en-la-cooperacion-sur-sur-el-caso-del-peru-y-colombia/.

Lo Lau, Jack. 2022. "Peru's ambassador to China: 'The FTA with China is becoming obsolete'." *Diálogo Chino* (1 July). https://dialogochino.net/en/trade-investment/55672-peru-china-trade-ambassador-fta-becoming-obsolete/.

Luna Mendoza, Víctor Ricardo. 2016. "Proyección internacional del Perú (2016–2021)." Mimeograph copy.

———. 2017. "Política exterior en un mundo de cambio." *La República* (14 July). Mimeograph copy.

———. 2022. "Gestión de Política Exterior Período, 2016–18." Mimeograph copy.

Lupu, Noam. 2012. "The 2011 general elections in Peru." *Electoral Studies* 31: 621–24. https://www.noamlupu.com/peru2011.pdf.

Marczak, Jason. 2010. "Peru's 'Look to Asia' Strategy Pays Off." *World Politics Review* (16 December). https://www.worldpoliticsreview.com/perus-look-to-asia-strategy-pays-off/.

Martínez, Alejandra Dinegro. 2022. "Peru: The Broken Dream of Transformative Government?" *NACLA Report on the Americas* (28 April). https://nacla.org/peru-broken-dream-transformative-government.

McClintock, Cynthia. 2006. "An Unlikely Comeback in Peru." *Journal of Democracy* 17, 4 (October): 95–109.

McClintock, Cynthia and Fabián Vallas. 2003. *The United States and Peru: Cooperation at a Cost*. London and New York: Routledge.

———. 2010. "The United States and Peru in the 2000s." In *Contemporary U.S.-Latin American Relations: Cooperation or Conflict in the 21st Century?* ed. Jorge I. Dominguez and Rafael Fernández de Castro, 197–217. London and New York: Routledge.

———. 2011. "Peru's Swing Left? Parsing the 2011 Elections." *Foreign Affairs* (June 23). https://www.foreignaffairs.com/articles/peru/2011-06-23/perus-swing-left.

Mijares, Víctor and Detlef Nolte. 2018. "Regionalismo posthegemónico en crisis ¿Por qué la Unasur se desintegra?" *Foreign Affairs Latinoamérica* 18, 3 (July-September): 105–12.

Ministerio de Relaciones Exteriores del Perú (MREP). 2006a. *Memoria institucional, agosto 2005-julio 2006*. Lima: Ministerio de Relaciones Exteriores.

———. 2006b. *Política exterior peruana, julio 2001-marzo 2006*. Lima: Ministerio de Relaciones Exteriores.

———. 2006c. *Un líder sin fronteras: Diplomacia presidencial, 2001–2006*. Lima: Oficina General de Comunicaciones.

———. 2009. *Delimitación Marítima entre el Perú y Chile*. Lima: Ministerio de Relaciones Exteriores.

———. 2011. *Memoria del Ministerio de Relaciones Exteriores, julio 2006–julio 2011*. Lima: Ministerio de Relaciones Exteriores. http://consulado.pe/politicaexterior/Documents/MEMORIA-del-MRE-Jul-2006-Jul2011.pdf.

———. 2013. *Memoria institucional del 28 de julio de 2011 al 15 de mayo del 2013*. Lima: Ministerio de Relaciones Exteriores. http://transparencia.rree.gob.pe/index.php/2-planeamiento-y-organizacion/2-5-memoria-institucional/8020-2-memoria-institucional-de-rafael-roncagliolo-orbegoso-2011-2013/file.

———. 2014. *Memoria institucional de 15 de mayo de 2013 al 24 de junio de 2014*. Lima: Ministerio de Relaciones Exteriores. https://xdoc.mx/preview/memoria-institucional-portal-de-transparencia-5e1f72eee2532.

———. 2015. *Información para la elaboración de la cuenta general de la república – ejercicio fiscal 2015*. Lima: Ministerio de Relaciones Exteriores.

———. 2017. *Memoria Anual 2016*. Lima: Ministerio de Relaciones Exteriores.

———. 2019a. *Memoria Anual 2018*. Lima: Ministerio de Relaciones Exteriores.

———. 2019b. "Pacto de Leticia por la Amazonía." Lima: Ministerio de Relaciones Exteriores. https://www.gob.pe/institucion/rree/noticias/50579-pacto-de-leticia-por-la-amazonia.

———. 2021a. "Discurso del Ministro de Relaciones Exteriores, Sr. Héctor Béjar Rivera, en la ceremonia de asunción del cargo." Lima: Ministerio de Relaciones Exteriores (2 August). https://www.gob.pe/institucion/rree/noticias/509162-discurso-del-ministro-de-relaciones-exteriores-sr-hector-bejar-rivera-en-la-ceremonia-de-asuncion-del-cargo.

———. 2021b. "Palabras del señor Canciller Embajador Oscar Maúrtua de Romaña en ceremonia de Asunción del Cargo de Ministro de Relaciones Exteriores." Lima: Ministerio de Relaciones Exteriores (24 August). https://www.gob.pe/institucion/rree/noticias/513225-palabras-del-senor-canciller-embajador-oscar-maurtua-de-romana-en-ceremonia-de-asuncion-del-cargo-de-ministro-de-relaciones-exteriores.

———. 2022. "Discurso del Canciller César Landa Arroyo en ceremonia de asunción del cargo de Ministro de Relaciones." Lima: Ministerio de Relaciones Exteriores (10 February). https://www.gob.pe/institucion/rree/noticias/582924-discurso-del-canciller-cesar-landa-arroyo-en-ceremonia-de-asuncion-del-cargo-de-ministro-de-relaciones-exteriores.

Moncada, Andrea. 2021. "What to Expect from Pedro Castillo." *Americas Quarterly* (10 June). https://americasquarterly.org/article/what-to-expect-from-pedro-castillo/.

Morimoto, Amelia. 1999. *Los japoneses y sus descendientes en el Perú*. Lima: Fondo Editorial del Congreso del Perú.

Namihas, Sandra. 2012. "La construcción de una asociación estratégica y un desarrollo fronterizo entre el Perú y Colombia." In *Veinte años de política exterior peruana (1991–2011)*, coordinator Fabián Novak, 53–74. Lima: Fondo Editorial de la Pontificia Universidad Católica del Perú.

———. 2016. "El inicio de 'las mil y una noches' de Turquía en América Latina y la visita de Erdogan al Perú." *Boletín Panorama Mundial IDEI* 8, 40.

Negro, Dante. 2012. "Las relaciones entre el Perú y la OEA (1991–2011)." In *Veinte años de política exterior peruana (1991–2011)*, coordinator Fabián Novak, 273–304. Lima: Fondo Editorial de la Pontificia Universidad Católica del Perú.

Nolte, Detlef and Leslie Wehner. 2013. "The Pacific Alliance Casts Its Cloud over Latin America." German Institute of Global and Area Studies (GIGA). Number 8. https://www.giga-hamburg.de/en/publications/giga-focus/the-pacific-alliance-casts-its-cloud-over-latin-america.

Novak, Fabián. 2000. *Las Conversaciones entre Perú y Chile para la Ejecución del Tratado de 1929.* Lima: Fondo Editorial de la Pontificia Universidad Católica del Perú.

———. 2012. "Las relaciones entre el Perú y Europa: Los casos de Alemania, España y Francia." In *Veinte años de política exterior peruana (1991–2011)*, coordinator Fabián Novak, 175–205. Lima: Fondo Editorial de la Pontificia Universidad Católica del Perú.

Novak, Fabián and Sandra Namihas. 2010. *Perú-Ecuador: Una experiencia exitosa de paz y buena vecindad.* Lima: Konrad Adenauer Stiftung and Instituto de Estudios Internacionales Pontificia Universidad Católica del Perú. https://repositorio.pucp.edu.pe/index/handle/123456789/39907.

———. 2012. *Las relaciones entre el Perú y Brasil (1826–2012).* Lima: Konrad Adenauer Stiftung and Instituto de Estudios Internationales Pontificia Universidad Católica del Perú. https://repositorio.pucp.edu.pe/index/handle/123456789/39910.

———. 2013. *La relaciones entre el Perú y Bolivia (1826–2013).* Lima: Konrad Adenauer Stiftung and Instituto de Estudios Internationales Pontificia Universidad Católica del Perú. https://repositorio.pucp.edu.pe/index/handle/123456789/39911.

———. 2016. *Las relaciones entre el Perú y la Unión Europea.* Lima: Konrad Adenauer Stiftung and Instituto de Estudios Internationales Pontificia Universidad Católica del Perú. https://repositorio.pucp.edu.pe/index/handle/123456789/133505.

———. 2018a. *La Alianza del Pacífico: Situación, Perspectivas y propuestas para su consolidación.* Lima: Konrad Adenauer Stiftung and Instituto de Estudios Internationales Pontificia Universidad Católica del Perú. https://repositorio.pucp.edu.pe/index/handle/123456789/53176.

———. 2018b. *The Foreign Policy of President Donald Trump and Its Impact on Latin America.* Lima: Konrad Adenauer Stiftung and Instituto de Estudios Internationales Pontificia Universidad Católica del Perú. https://repositorio.pucp.edu.pe/index/handle/123456789/134500.

———. 2020. *El bicentenario de la política exterior peruana y su projección en un mundo de cambios.* Lima: Konrad Adenauer Stiftung and Instituto de Estudios Internationales Pontificia Universidad Católica del Perú.

Organization of American States (OAS). 2017. "'Governabilidad democrática frente a la corrupción' será el tema de la Cumbre de las Américas de Perú 2018." Comunicado de Prensa (20 June). https://www.oas.org/es/centro_noticias/comunicado_prensa.asp?sCodigo=C-048/17.

———. 2018. "Compromiso de Lima: Governabilidad Democrática Frente a la Corrupción." VIII Cumbre de las Américas. Lima, Peru (13–14 April). http://www.summit-americas.org/LIMA_COMMITMENT/LimaCommitment_es.pdf.

Palacio, Juan Ferdinand. 2020. "¿Distracción o norte? La convergencia Alianza del Pacífico-MERCOSUR." Real Instituto El Cano (3 February). https://www.realinstitutoelcano.org/analisis/distraccion-o-norte-la-convergencia-alianza-del-pacifico-mercosur/#:~:text=En.

Palacios Rodríguez, Raúl. 1974. *La Chilenización de Tacna y Arica, 1883–1929.* Lima: Editorial Arica.

Palma Valderrama, Hugo Ernesto. 2022. "Embajador in Ecuador." Lima. Mimeograph.

Palmer, David Scott. 1995. "Peru's 1995 Elections: A Second Look." *LASA Forum* 26, 2 (Summer): 17–20.

———. 1998. "Relaciones entre Estados Unidos y el Perú durante el decenio de 1990: dinámicas, antecedentes y proyecciones." *Política Internacional* 53 (July/September): 23–45.

Paz, Christian. 2020. "The Biden Doctrine Begins with Latin America." *The Atlantic* (20 October). https://www.theatlantic.com/international/archive/2020/10/joe-biden-foreign-policy-latin-america/616841/.

Paz-Soldan, Gabriela. 2022. "Castillo's Turmoil: How Institutions Hamper Peru's New Leader." *Brown Political Review* (25 March).

Pérez de Cuéllar, Javier. 2012. *Memorias: Recuerdos personales y políticos.* Lima: Aguilar.

Philip, George and Francisco Panizza. 2011. *The Triumph of Politics: The Return of the Left in Venezuela, Bolivia and Ecuador.* Cambridge, UK: Polity.

Popolizio Bardales, Néstor. 2019. "Interview: Néstor Popolizio." *The Report: Peru 2019.* London: Oxford Business Group.

———. 2022. "Gestión de política exterior period 2018–2019." Lima, Peru. August. Mimeograph copy.

Portales, Carlos. 2012. "CELAC: a voice for Latin America and the Caribbean?" NOREF [Norwegian Peacebuilding Resource Centre] Report (February). https://www.files.ethz.ch/isn/137613/CELAC.pdf.

Prado, Josefina del. 2015. "Política exterior del Perú en la Comunidad Andina." In *La política exterior peruana en el siglo XXI: Agenda y propuestas,* coordinator Fabián Novak and Jaime García, 159–74. Lima: Fondo Editorial de la Pontificia Universidad Católica del Perú and Konrad Adenauer Stiftung.

Quiroz, Alfonso W. 2008. *Corrupt Circles: A History of Unbound Graft in Peru.* Washington, D.C.: Woodrow Wilson Center Press and Baltimore, MD: Johns Hopkins University Press.

Ramacciotti, Beatriz and María Méndez. 2012. "Las relaciones entre Perú y Estados Unidos: Dos décadas de asociación convergente." In *Veinte años de política exterior peruana (1991–2011),* coordinator Fabián Novak, 95–140. Lima: Fondo Editorial de la Pontificia Universidad Católica del Perú.

Ramírez Bullón, Javier Ernesto and Lizeth Vanessa Ayala Castiblanco. 2017. "China's importance in the foreign policy of Colombia and Peru: A Comparative perspective." Paper presented at ISA 58th Annual Conference, Baltimore (February). Mimeograph copy.

Ratigan, Kerry. 2021. "Are Peruvians Enticed by the 'China Model'?" *Studies in Comparative International Development* 56, 2 (March): 87–111.

Renique, Gerardo. 2013. "Peru: Humala Submits to the United States and the Mining Industry." *NACLA Report on the Americas* 46, 3: 12–17. https://nacla.org/article/peru-humala-submits-united-states-and-mining-industry.

Rodríguez Cuadros, José Manuel. 2007. *Delimitación marítima con equidad: El caso de Perú y Chile.* Lima: Ediciones PEISA.

———. 2021. "El servicio diplomático y el bicentenario." *RPP Noticias* (23 February). https://rpp.pe/columnistas/manuelrodriguezcuadros/el-servicio-diplomatico-y-el-bicentenario-noticia-1322435.

Roncagliolo, Santiago. 2018. *La Cuarta Espada: La historia de Abimael Guzmán y Sendero Luminoso.* Barcelona: Penguin Random House.

St John, Ronald Bruce. 1976. "The End of Innocence: Peruvian Foreign Policy and the United States, 1919–1942." *Journal of Latin American Studies* 8, 2 (November): 325–44.

———. 1992. *The Foreign Policy of Peru.* Boulder, CO: Lynne Rienner.

———. 1994. *The Bolivia-Chile-Peru Dispute in the Atacama Desert.* International Boundaries Research Unit, University of Durham, Boundary and Territory Briefing, 1 (6). https://www.durham.ac.uk/research/institutes-and-centres/ibru-borders-research/maps-and-publications/publications/publications-catalogue/the-bolivia-chile-peru-dispute-in-the-atacama-desert.php.

———. 1996. "Peru: Atypical External Behavior." In *Foreign Policy & Regionalism in the Americas*, ed. Gordon Mace and Jean-Philippe Thérien, 121–36. Boulder, CO: Lynne Rienner.

———. 1999a. *Ecuador-Peru Boundary Dispute: The Road to Settlement*, International Boundaries Research Unit, University of Durham, Boundary and Territory Briefing, 3 (1). https://www.durham.ac.uk/media/durham-university/research-/research-centres/ibru-centre-for-borders-research/maps-and-databases/publications-database/boundary-amp-territory-briefings/btb_3-1.pdf.

———. 1999b. *La política exterior del Perú.* Lima: Asociación de Funcionarios del Servicio Diplomático del Perú.

———. 2000. "Chile, Peru and the Treaty of 1929: The Final Settlement." *IBRU Boundary and Security Bulletin*, 8, 1 : 91–100. https://duracuk-lb01-production.terminalfour.net/media/durham-university/research-/research-centres/ibru-centre-for-borders-research/maps-and-databases/publications-database/boundary-amp-security-bulletins/bsb8-1_john.pdf.

———. 2003. "New Solutions to Old Problems in Latin America." *Foreign Policy in Focus* (22 May).

———. 2006a. "Evo Morales No Che Guevara." *Foreign Policy in Focus* (9 January).

———. 2006b. "Peru's Humala is Washington's Next 'Worst Nightmare'." *Foreign Policy in Focus* (25 April).

———. 2006c. "Politics of Peru in Flux." *Foreign Policy in Focus* (29 June).

———. 2006d. "García's First 100 Days." *Foreign Policy in Focus* (28 November).

———. 2010. *Toledo's Peru: Vision and Reality.* Gainesville: University Press of Florida.

———. 2016. "The Peruvian Response to the Rise of Brazil: Developing a Strategic Relationship." In *Foreign Policy Responses to the Rise of Brazil: Balancing Power in Emerging States*, ed. Gian Luca Gardini and Maria Herminia Tavares de Almeida, 145–59. Houndmills, Basingstoke, Hampshire: Palgrave Macmillan.

———. 2017. "Peruvian foreign policy in the new millennium: Continuity and change." *Revista del Instituto Riva-Agüero (RIRA)* 2, 2 (October): 65–119.

———. 2020. *Bolivia: Geopolitics of a Landlocked State.* London and New York: Routledge.

———. 2022. "Peru: A Model for Latin American Diplomacy and Statecraft." In *Routledge Handbook of Diplomacy and Statecraft*, Second edition, ed. B. J. C. Mckercher, 198–209. London and New York: Routledge.

Sánchez, Wilder Alejandro. 2012. "Commentary: Peru Finds Itself Snared in the Falklands/Malvinas Dispute." Council on Foreign Relations (29 April). https://www.coha.org/commentary-troubled-peru-and-the-falklandsmalvinas-dispute/.

———. 2014. "Misiones singularmente complicadas: El rol del Perú en las operaciones de paz de las Naciones Unidas." *Perspectivas* 2: 7–19.

Sánchez, Wilder Alejandro and Otto Raúl Tielmans Jr. 2015. "Reinvigorating Peru's role in Antarctic geopolitics." *Polar Journal* 5, 1: 101–12.

Sánchez Vargas de Ríos and Ana María Liliana. 2016. "Balance la política exterior del gobierno, 2011–2016." Charla Magistral de la Ministra de Relaciones Exteriores, Ana María Sánchez de Ríos, Inaugurando el Año Lectivo de la Academia Diplomática del Perú (martes 29 de marzo de 2016). Lima. 29 March. Mimeograph copy.

Segovia Hernández, Daniela. 2013. "Latin America and the Caribbean: Between the OAS and CELAC." *European Review of Latin American and Caribbean Studies* 95 (October): 97–107.

Seoane Flores, Alfredo V. 2000. "Estado actual y proyecciones de la Comunidad Andina de Naciones." In *Bolivia: Temas de la agenda internacional*, coordinator Alberto Zelada Castedo, 291–312. La Paz: Ministerio de Relaciones y Culto. Zelada.

Shifter, Michael. 2021. "Peru's Fraying Democracy: Crisis Has Produced Only Bad Political Options." *Foreign Affairs* (3 June). https://www.foreignaffairs.com/articles/americas/2021-06-03/perus-fraying-democracy.

Sonneland, Holly K. 2022. "Six Notable Pedro Castillo Quotes as He Hits Six Months in Office." American Society/Council of the Americas (AS/COA) (27 January). https://www.as-coa.org/articles/six-notable-pedro-castillo-quotes-he-hits-six-months-office.

Stevens, Christopher and Others. 2012. "European Union: Trade Agreement with Colombia and Peru." Directorate-General for External Policy, Policy Department. https://intranet.eulacfoundation.org/en/system/files/EU%20Trade%20agreement%20with%20Colombia%20and%20Peru.pdf.

Stewart, Watt. 1951. *Chinese Bondage in Peru: A History of the Chinese Coolie in Peru, 1849–1874*). Durham, NC: Duke University Press.

Stone, Alex. 2002. "A Wayward Path: The Failure of US Policy in Peru." *Harvard International Review* 23, 4 (January): 45–49.

Stuenkel, Oliver. 2018. "The 2018 Summit of the Americas: A Lost Opportunity." Council of Councils (23 April). https://www.cfr.org/councilofcouncils/global-memos/2018-summit-americas-lost-opportunity.

Sweigart, Emilie. 2022. "Peru and Pedro Castillo: An Overview." *Americas Quarterly* (3 May). https://www.americasquarterly.org/article/peru-and-pedro-castillo-an-overview/.

Sweigart, Emilie and Gabriel Cohen. 2021. "Peru's Evolving Relationship with China." *Americas Quarterly* (19 October). https://www.americasquarterly.org/article/perus-evolving-relationship-with-china/.

Tanaka, Martín. 1998. *Los Espejismos de la Democracia: El colapso del sistema de partidos en el Perú, 1980–1995*. Lima: Instituto de Estudios Peruanos.

———. 2001. ¿Crónica de una muerte anunciada? Determinismo, voluntarismo, actors y poderes estructurales en el Perú." In *Lecciones del final del fujimorismo*, ed. Jane Marcus-Delgado and Martín Tanaka, 57–112. Lima: Instituto de Estudios Peruanos.

Tapia Samaniego, Hildebrando. 2011. *Peruanos en el exterior.* Lima: Fondo Editorial del Congreso del Perú.

Tegel, Simeon. 2017. "Peru's Opposition Plays Hardball." *Americas Quarterly* (13 June). https://www.americasquarterly.org/article/perus-opposition-plays-hardball/.

Toledo Manrique, Alejandro Celestino. 2001. "Mensaje del president constitucional del Perú, doctor Alejandro Toledo Manrique, ante el Congreso Nacional, el 28 de julio de 2001." Lima. https://www.congreso.gob.pe/Docs/participacion/museo/congreso/files/mensajes/2001-2020/files/mensaje-2005-at.pdf.

Toledo Orozco, Zaraí. 2019. "Peru Dissolves Congress, Setting Up a Fight for the Political Future." *NACLA Report on the Americas* (5 November). https://nacla.org/news/2019/11/04/peru-congress-vizcarra.

Tudela van Breugel Douglas, Francisco. 2019. "Una estrategia para la paz: Diseño y desarrollo de las negociaciones peruano-ecuatorianas 1995–1997." In *El proceso de negociaciones entre el Perú y el Ecuador (1995–1998) y los 20 años de los Acuerdos de Paz de Brasilia*, coordinator Néstor Popolizio, 95–113. Lima: Konrad Adenauer Stiftung, Ministerio de Relaciones del Perú and Pontificia Universidad Católica del Perú.

Ugarteche, Pedro. 1930. *La política internacional peruana durante la dictadura de Leguía*. Lima: C.A. Castrillón.

United Nations Environment Programme (UNEP). 2022. "Draft Resolution from Rwanda and Peru on an International Legally Binding Instrument on Plastic Pollution, 10 Jan 2022." UNEP (11 January). https://wedocs.unep.org/handle/20.500.11822/37808.

United States of America. 2022a. "Secretary Antony J. Blinken and Peruvian Foreign Minister César Landa at a Joint Press Availability." Lima (7 October). https://www.state.gov/secretary-antony-j-blinken-and-peruvian-foreign-minister-cesar-landa-at-a-joint-press-availability/.

———. 2022b. "Project 'Por la Pesca' (For Fishing) Seeks to Help Artisanal Fishing and Will Promote Sustainable Fishing." Lima (17 October). https://pe.usembassy.gov/united-states-launches-alliance-to-fight-illegal-unreported-and-unregulated-fishing-in-peru-and-ecuador/#:~:text=Antony%20Blinken%2C%20Secretary%20of%20State,fishing%20in%20Ecuador%20and%20Peru.

Valdez Carrillo, Jorge. 2012. "Las relaciones del Perú con la Europa Comunitaria." In *Veinte años de política exterior peruana (1991–2011)*, coordinator Fabián Novak, 161–74. Lima: Fondo Editorial de la Pontificia Universidad Católica del Perú.

Valladares, Ivan. 2016. "PPK's Divisive Tactics." Council on Hemispheric Affairs (3 July). https://www.coha.org/ppks-divisive-tactics/.

Vergara, Alberto. 2022. "An Eruption of History in Peru's Bicentenary." *Current History* 121, 832 (1 February): 857–62.

Wagner de Reyna, Alberto. 1964. *Historia diplomática del Perú (1900–1945)*, 2 vols. Lima: Ediciones Peruanas.

Wieland Conroy, Hubert. 2017. "El punto *Concordia* y la frontera entre el Perú y Chile." Lima: Instituto de Estudios Internacionales Pontificia Universidad Católica del Perú.

Winter, Brian. 2020. "The Backlash to Venezuelan Migration Is Here." *Americas Quarterly* (20 April). https://www.americasquarterly.org/article/the-backlash-to-venezuelan-migration-is-here/.

———. 2022. "What the Summit of the Americas Mess Really Tells Us." *Americas Quarterly* (12 May). https://www.americasquarterly.org/article/what-the-summit-of-the-americas-mess-really-tells-us/.

Youngers, Coletta A. 2006. "Promoting Human Rights: NGOs and the State in Peru." In *Making Institutions Work in Peru*, ed. John Crabtree, 158–84. London: Institute for the Study of the Americas.

Zanabria, Luzmila. 2015. "Las relaciones entre el Perú y China." In *La política exterior peruana en el siglo XXI: Agenda y propuestas*, coordinator Fabián Novak and Jaime García, 87–99. Lima: Fondo Editorial de la Pontificia Universidad Católica del Perú and Konrad Adenauer Stiftung.

Interviews

Álvarez Rodrich, Augusto. 2008. Journalist and editor (*Perú21*). Lima, Peru, 12 March.
Araníbar Quiroga, Antonio. 2001. Foreign Minister of Bolivia (1993–97). La Paz, Bolivia, 13 March.
Arróspide del Busto, José Antonio. 2008. Executive Director of the Perú-Ecuador Binational Development Plan (2006–10). Lima, Peru, 13 March.
Belaúnde Terry, Fernando. 1969, 1983. President of Peru (1963–68, 1980–85). Denver, Colorado, 16 May 1969, Lima, Peru, 11 July 1983.
De la Puente Radbill, José Carlos. 2003. Foreign Minister of Peru (July 1976–January 1979). Lima, Peru, 9 May.
De Trazegnies Granda, Fernando. 1999. Foreign Minister of Peru (October 1998– November 2000). Lima, Peru, 2 September.
Flores Nano, Lourdes. 2003, 2008. Lawyer, Politician, Congresswoman. Lima, Peru, 30 April 2003, 13 March 2008.
García Belaúnde, José Antonio. 2014. Foreign Minister of Peru (2006–11). Lima, Peru, 14 January.
García-Sayán Larrabure, Diego. 2008. Foreign Minister of Peru (2001–2002). Lima, Peru, 11 March.
Gumucio Granier, Jorge. 1999, 2001. Bolivian Ambassador to Peru (1994–2000), Deputy Foreign Minister of Bolivia (2004–2006). Lima, Peru, 1 September 1999, La Paz, Bolivia, 13 March 2001.
Luna Mendoza, Víctor Ricardo. 1999, 2022. Foreign Minister of Peru (2016–18), Ambassador to the United States (1992–99). Lima, Peru, 1 September 1999; via-email, 15 June 2022, 28 June 2022, 7 July 2022, 24 July 2022, 5 August 2022.
Maúrtua de Romaña, Óscar. 1983, 2006. Secretary General to President Fernando Belaúnde Terry (1980–85), Foreign Minister of Peru (August 2005–July 2006, August 2021– February 2022). Lima, Peru, 11 July 1983, 18 April 2006.
Palma Valderrama, Hugo Ernesto. 1999, 2006. Ambassador to Japan (2006–2008). Deputy Foreign Minister of Peru (1991, 1997–98). Lima, Peru, 1 September 1999, 20 April 2006.
Paniagua Corazao, Valentín. 2001. President of Peru (November 2000–July 2001). Lima, Peru, 16 March.
Pérez de Cuéllar Guerra, Javier. 1999, 2001. Secretary-General of the United Nations (1982–92), Prime Minister and Foreign Minister of Peru (2000–2001). Lima, Peru, 31 August 1999, 14 March 2001.
Rodríguez Cuadros, José Manuel. 2003, 2008. Deputy Foreign Minister of Peru (July 2001– December 2003), Foreign Minister of Peru (December 2003–August 2005). Lima, Peru, 30 April 2003, 14 March 2008.
Roncagliolo Orbegoso, Rafael. 2014. Foreign Minister of Peru (July 2011–May 2013). Lima, Peru, via e-mail, 20 October.
Sánchez de Lozada, Gonzalo. 2003. President of Bolivia (1993–97, 2002–2003). Bloomington, Illinois, 9 September.
Toledo Manrique, Alejandro Celestino. 2003, 2006, 2008, 2009. President of Peru (2001–2006) Lima, Peru, 9 May 2003, 19 April 2006; Palo Alto, California, 12 September 2008; via telephone, 10 July, 20 July, 28 July, 10 August 2009; via e-mail, 28 August 2009.

Tudela van Breugel-Douglas, Francisco. 1999. Foreign Minister of Peru (July 1995–July 1997), First Vice President of Peru (July 2000–November 2000). Lima, Peru, 31 August.

Villanueva, Víctor. 1983. Academic. Lima, Peru, 14 July.

Wagner Tizón, Allan. 2003. Foreign Minister of Peru (July 1985–May 1988, July 2002–December 2003, February 2021–July 2021). Lima, Peru, 9 May.

Newspapers and Other Media

Agence France-Presse (*AFP*) (Paris, France)
Andina (Lima, Peru)
Associated Press (*AP*) (New York, New York)
BBC News (*BBC*) (London)
Bloomberg (New York, New York)
Caretas (Lima, Peru)
CNN Español (Atlanta, Georgia)
El Comercio (Lima, Peru)
El Diario (La Paz, Bolivia)
Economist (London, England)
Expreso (Lima, Peru)
Gestión (Lima, Peru)
Merco Press (Montevideo, Uruguay)
Miami Herald (Miami, Florida)
New York Times (*NYT*) (New York, New York)
New York Times en Español (New York, New York)
El Peruano (Lima, Peru)
Perú21 (Lima, Peru)
RPP Noticias (Lima, Peru)
La Razón (La Paz, Bolivia)
La República (Lima, Peru)
Reuters (London, England)
Washington Post (*WP*) (Washington, DC)

INDEX